READING QUEST

Motinceanu

EXPERT

A Faithful Guide Through
Your Reading Adventures

DARAKWON

Radu Hadrian Hotinceanu
- MFA degree in Creative Writing from Arizona State University
- BA degree in English & Rhetoric from State University of New York at Binghamton
- Professor of English Language and Literature at Seoul Women's University
- Over 20 years of teaching experience at universities in Korea
- English language editor of *ASIANA Airlines In-flight Magazine*
- Former English language editor of *SPACE* and *Diplomacy* magazines

READING QUEST `EXPERT`

Author	Radu Hadrian Hotinceanu
Publisher	Chung Kyudo
Editors	Kwon Minjeong, Cho Sangik
Designers	Hwang Sooyoung, Jeong Hyunseok
Photo Credits	pg. 18 (Spider-Man) Trismegist san / Shutterstock.com; pg. 19 (Japanese Anime Cosplay) Tofudevil / Shutterstock.com; pg. 23 (Superman and Goku) Krikkiat / Shutterstock.com; pg. 40-41 (Stan Lee) Jaguar PS / Shutterstock.com; pg. 42 (Above: comics *Fantastic Four*) emka74 / Shutterstock.com, (Below: Marvel superheroes) Anton_Ivanov / Shutterstock.com; pg. 43 (Hulk) Anton_Ivanov / Shutterstock.com; pg. 50 (Atari retro console) Tinxi / Shutterstock.com; pg. 51 (the Fairchild Channel F) Gary L Hider / Shutterstock.com; pg. 56-57 (a vintage Ferrari) ermess / Shutterstock.com; pg. 58 (Above: Alfa Romeo) Karolis Kavolelis / Shutterstock.com, (Below: the Olympic torch) lexan / Shutterstock.com; pg. 59 (a yellow Ferrari) Fede Desal / Shutterstock.com; pg. 63 (Pininfarina Battista) Art Konovalov / Shutterstock.com; pg. 64-65 (a BVLGARI store) Chrispictures / Shutterstock.com; pg. 66 (BVLGARI products) DELBO ANDREA / Shutterstock.com; pg. 67 (BVLGARI Serpenti jewelry) Svetlana Timonina / Shutterstock.com; pg. 71 (Julianne Moore) s_bukley / Shutterstock.com; pg. 72-73 (David Bowie) Anton_Ivanov / Shutterstock.com; pg. 74 (Luke Spiller performs on stage) Debby Wong / Shutterstock.com; pg. 75 (American rock band Kiss) Tony Norkus / Shutterstock.com; pg. 82 (statue of Giacomo Puccini) AlexMastro / Shutterstock.com; pg. 83 (Scenes from *La Bohème* and *Turandot*) Igor Bulgarin / Shutterstock.com; pg. 87 (sketch of Puccini) Natata / Shutterstock.com; pg. 106 (Ovidiu Square) Mitzo / Shutterstock.com; pg. 107 (a stamp) irisphoto1 / Shutterstock.com; pg. 115 (Juan Rulfo) public domain / Wikimedia.org

First Published in November 2020
By Darakwon Inc.
Darakwon Bldg., 211, Munbal-ro, Paju-si, Gyeonggi-do 10881
Republic of Korea
Tel: 82-2-736-2031 (Ext. 552)

Price	15,000 won
ISBN	978-89-277-0985-5 14740
	978-89-277-0969-5 14740 (set)

www.darakwon.co.kr

Components	Main Book / Free MP3 Recordings Available Online
	7 6 5 4 3 2 1 20 21 22 23 24

To the Readers

Reading Quest Expert is the third book in a three-book series of readers for adult learners of English. This series contains readings that range from a high-beginning to a high-advanced level. All three books in the series were written with the goal of presenting readings that are interesting, fun, and level appropriate.

Reading Quest Expert is divided into seven units that explore the topics of world culture, space travel, 20th century visionaries, industrial design, music, ethics for the 21st century, and literary figures. Each unit presents two current and engaging stories on a topic. These reading passages are previewed in a Unit Preview section and are further explored in Reading Comprehension, Proofreading and Writing Practice, Vocabulary in Context, and Reading Connections sections.

The discussion activities in the Unit Preview make this section ideal for classroom use. The Reading Comprehension section emphasizes the development of reading skills such as searching for details and identifying the main topic. The Proofreading and Writing Practice section focuses on error correction and gives readers the opportunity for writing a paragraph on the topic of the lesson presented. The Vocabulary in Context section focuses on word analysis skills such as determining the contextual usage of words and understanding the use of phrasal expressions. Lastly, the Reading Connections section provides further information that is relevant to the topic, giving readers the chance to extend their understanding of the reading passages.

Radu Hadrian Hotinceanu

CONTENTS

UNIT ELEMENTS

Each unit of *Reading Quest Expert* includes the following sections and features:

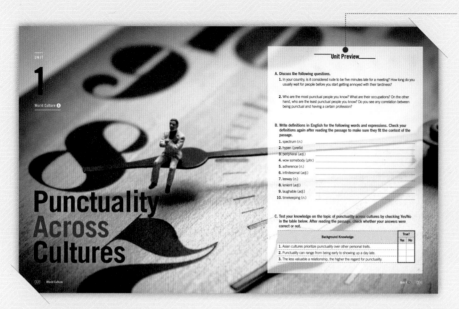

◀ Unit Preview

Three types of activities prepare readers for the reading passage: warm-up questions, vocabulary definitions, and background knowledge questions. The unit preview activities create reader engagement and increase understanding of the reading passage.

◀ Usage and Etymology

This section explains the origins and meanings of two idioms or expressions from the reading passage.

Reading Passages ▶

Each reading passage has the appropriate sentence length and complexity for the low-advanced to high-advanced level.

What Did They Mean? ▶

Quotations by famous people are provided in the margins of the reading passage in order to encourage readers to reflect on the presented topic from unique, metaphorically written perspectives.

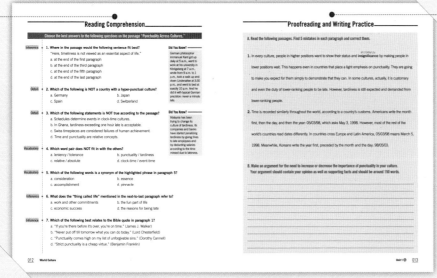

Proofreading and Writing Practice

Proofreading exercises focus on grammatical and vocabulary corrections. The writing practice gives readers the chance to write a paragraph in their own words.

Reading Comprehension

A set of comprehension questions helps readers test their understanding of the key information of the reading passage.

Vocabulary in Context

Different types of vocabulary exercises provide practice in using the unit's vocabulary in practical contexts.

Reading Connections

Every unit includes an additional reading on a topic related to the unit's reading passage. It extends readers' knowledge and provides them with the opportunity for further reflection on the subject.

Did You Know?

Fun facts related to the reading passage are presented in a box format on the side of the activities in the Reading Comprehension and Vocabulary in Context sections.

Punctuality Across Cultures

Unit Preview

A. Discuss the following questions.

1. In your country, is it considered rude to be five minutes late for a meeting? How long do you usually wait for people before you start getting annoyed with their tardiness?

2. Who are the most punctual people you know? What are their occupations? On the other hand, who are the least punctual people you know? Do you see any correlation between being punctual and having a certain profession?

B. Write definitions in English for the following words and expressions. Check your definitions again after reading the passage to make sure they fit the context of the passage.

1. spectrum (*n.*) ....
2. hyper- (*prefix*) ....
3. peripheral (*adj.*) ....
4. wow somebody (*phr.*) ....
5. adherence (*n.*) ....
6. infinitesimal (*adj.*) ....
7. leeway (*n.*) ....
8. lenient (*adj.*) ....
9. laughable (*adj.*) ....
10. timekeeping (*n.*) ....

C. Test your knowledge on the topic of punctuality across cultures by checking Yes/No in the table below. After reading the passage, check whether your answers were correct or not.

Background Knowledge	True?	
	Yes	No
1. Asian cultures prioritize punctuality over other personal traits.		
2. Punctuality can range from being early to showing up a day late.		
3. The less valuable a relationship, the higher the regard for punctuality.		

01

"There is an appointed time for everything, a time for every activity under the heavens." (Ecclesiastes 3:1) This Bible verse that served as a caution for farmers to plant their crops at the proper time if they wished to yield good results implies, in a more contemporary sense, that punctuality will yield good

Punctuality is a relative concept.

results. The concept of punctuality, it seems, has been around for quite some time.

Punctuality, however, much like time itself, is a relative concept. If Einstein proved to us the relativity of time, numerous cultures around the world have taught us that punctuality is a concept whose significance differs greatly, depending on where you live or who you ask.

Social psychologist Robert Levine determined that we can divide the world's cultures into those that live on "event time"—where events determine a person's schedule—and those that live on "clock time"—where events are determined by a person's schedule. At one end of the spectrum are hyper-punctual clock-time countries such as Germany, Switzerland, and Japan. At the opposite end are event-time countries such as Ghana, Ecuador, and Indonesia, where punctuality is at best a peripheral consideration.

But what does it really mean to be punctual? How many seconds or minutes—or hours for that matter—determine whether you've just wowed somebody with your strict adherence to the appointment time or terribly disappointed that person with your inexcusable tardiness?

In Switzerland, where masterfully engineered timepieces are held up at the high-water mark of all human achievement[1], it is perfectly normal to expect that every second is vital. The same can be said of Japan, where the *Shinkansen* (bullet) trains have an average delay of an infinitesimal 55 seconds... per year! In Germany,

What did they mean?

1 Explain the following George Bernard Shaw quote: "Better never than late."

What did they mean?

2 Explain the following Oscar Wilde quote: "Punctuality is the thief of time."

meanwhile, you are actually expected to be early for a meeting.

In countries such as Canada, the United States, or the UK, most people— though not all—will give you a bit of leeway when it comes to timeliness; think a few minutes at the most. After all, Americans will tell you, "Time is money," so how much money can one just freely give away?

In other countries, views regarding punctuality are more lenient. Being half an hour late is still considered being on time in Belgium, France, Norway, and parts of Asia. Meanwhile, in Italy, Spain, and parts of Latin America, the leniency extends up to one hour.

Then there are the countries where the idea that a person's life should be ruled by the clock is laughable. In Ghana, if you've arrived at 3 p.m. for a 10 a.m. meeting, you're on time somehow. Not to mention the infamous "Moroccan time," which allows for a tardiness of up to a full day... well, depending on who you are supposed to meet.

Strict punctuality does yield good results, as the Bible rightfully points out. After all, there is a definite connection between the clock-time culture and the economic success of countries such as Germany, Japan, the UK, and the United States. But sometimes there is this thing called life that gets in the way of punctuality. One might ask where the fun of always being on time is. It is one of those things that goes deep with[2] Greek, Irish, and other fun-loving cultures.

In cross-cultural timekeeping, one rule seems to hold true whenever we discuss degrees of punctuality: the more valuable the relationship with the person one is meeting, the higher the regard for punctuality. After all, no Moroccan citizen would be even a second late for a meeting with the Moroccan king.

35

What did they mean?

3 Explain the following Evelyn Waugh quote: "Punctuality is the virtue of the bored."

40

45

50

55

→ **IDIOMS: Usage and Etymology** ←

1 **to be held up at the high-water mark of all human achievement:** The "high-water mark" literally means the mark left when a body of water reaches its highest point, as it would during a flood. The term started being used in a figurative sense in the 19th century, when it took the meaning of "the highest point or the apex of something." The idiom therefore means "to be considered the highest level of human achievement."

2 **It is one of those things that goes deep with people:** The idiom means, in a figurative way, that "it is a thing that people care deeply about." The idiom is based on the expression "to go/run deep," as in "Pride goes/runs deep in this small town," meaning that "pride is felt strongly—and has been around for a long time—in this small town."

Reading Comprehension

Choose the best answers to the following questions on the passage "Punctuality Across Cultures."

Inference

1. Where in the passage would the following sentence fit best?

"Here, timeliness is not viewed as an essential aspect of life."

a. at the end of the first paragraph

b. at the end of the third paragraph

c. at the end of the fifth paragraph

d. at the end of the last paragraph

Detail

2. Which of the following is NOT a country with a hyper-punctual culture?

a. Germany

b. Japan

c. Spain

d. Switzerland

Detail

3. Which of the following statements is NOT true according to the passage?

a. Schedules determine events in clock-time cultures.

b. In Ghana, tardiness exceeding one hour late is acceptable.

c. Swiss timepieces are considered failures of human achievement.

d. Time and punctuality are relative concepts.

Vocabulary

4. Which word pair does NOT fit in with the others?

a. leniency / tolerance

b. punctuality / tardiness

c. relative / absolute

d. clock-time / event-time

Vocabulary

5. Which of the following words is a synonym of the highlighted phrase in paragraph 5?

a. consideration

b. essence

c. accomplishment

d. pinnacle

Inference

6. What does the "thing called life" mentioned in the next-to-last paragraph refer to?

a. work and other commitments

b. the fun part of life

c. economic success

d. the reasons for being late

Inference

7. Which of the following best relates to the Bible quote in paragraph 1?

a. "If you're there before it's over, you're on time." (James J. Walker)

b. "Never put off till tomorrow what you can do today." (Lord Chesterfield)

c. "Punctuality comes high on my list of unforgivable sins." (Dorothy Cannell)

d. "Strict punctuality is a cheap virtue." (Benjamin Franklin)

Did You Know? ∞∞∞∞∞∞∞∞

German philosopher Immanuel Kant got up daily at 5 a.m., went to work at his university in Königsberg at 7 a.m., wrote from 9 a.m. to 1 p.m., took a walk up and down Lindenallee at 3:30 p.m., and went to bed at exactly 10 p.m. And he did it with typical German precision: never a minute late.

Did You Know? ∞∞∞∞∞∞∞∞

Malaysia has been trying to change its culture of tardiness. Its companies and banks have started penalizing tardiness by giving fines to late employees and by deducting salaries according to the time missed due to lateness.

Proofreading and Writing Practice

A. Read the following passages. Find 5 mistakes in each paragraph and correct them.

1. In every culture, people in higher positions want to show their status and ~~insignificance~~ *importance* by making people in lower positions wait. This happens even in countries that place a light emphasis on punctuality. They are going to make you expect for them simply to demonstrate that they can. In some cultures, actually, it is customary and even the duty of lower-ranking people to be late. However, tardiness is still expected and demanded from lower-ranking people.

2. Time is recorded similarly throughout the world, according to a country's customs. Americans write the month first, then the day, and then the year: 05/03/98, which asks May 3, 1998. However, most of the rest of the world's countries read dates differently. In countries cross Europe and Latin America, 05/03/98 means March 5, 1998. Meanwhile, Koreans write the year first, preceded by the month and the day: 98/05/03.

B. Make an argument for the need to increase or decrease the importance of punctuality in your culture. Your argument should contain your opinion as well as supporting facts and should be around 150 words.

Vocabulary in Context

A. Complete the conversation below with vocabulary from the passage.

leeway	hyper	wow	laughable	infinitesimal	lenient

A: You've been _____ [1]-sensitive these past few days. Is everything okay?

B: I don't know. I feel so insignificant, so _____ [2]...

A: Uh-oh. You're getting philosophical again, aren't you?

B: Maybe to you it's _____ [3] that I think of life all the time, but I can't help it. I just get so anxious about my place in life.

A: No, I get it. It's who you are. But give yourself some _____ [4], and don't think about the serious stuff all the time. Have some fun, too.

B: I know. I wish I could be more _____ [5] with myself, but I have so many expectations to deal with.

A: Are you trying to _____ [6] the whole world?

B: Just myself. Impressing others is not too high on my wish list.

Did You Know?

George Washington took his dinners at exactly 4 p.m. When he invited members of Congress to dine with him and they arrived late, he would finish his dinner alone and say to the tardy guests, "We are punctual here. My cook never asks whether the company has arrived but whether the hour has come."

B. Choose the sentences where the underlined words have the same meanings as they do in the passage.

1. a. Let's put aside the peripheral issues and focus on the main ones.

 b. A monitor is a peripheral device on a computer.

2. a. The veterinarian took great caution in treating my pet canary.

 b. The professor's speech was a caution against complacency.

3. a. All employees must follow a strict adherence to rules and regulations.

 b. Unfortunately, this paint's adherence to wood is not uniform.

C. Complete the chart below with definitions for the given phrases using "run." Then, write sentences using the phrases.

Phrases	Definitions
1. run deep in	*it is very important to*
2. in the long run	
3. run around in circles	
4. run a fever	
5. a dry run	

Did You Know?

Allegrophobia is the intense fear of being late for a meeting or a scheduled event. The phobia comes with the compulsion to make excessive plans in order to ensure punctuality.

1. *Patriotism and the sense of sacrifice for one's country* **run deep in** *military families.*

2. _____

3. _____

4. _____

5. _____

Read the following passage on the Protestant work ethic. Then, do the exercises.

The Protestant Work Ethic

🎧 02

Why is punctuality so important to northern Europeans and other traditionally Protestant cultures? To understand their obsession with timekeeping, we must understand the Protestant work ethic, a term coined by German economic sociologist Max Weber (1864-1920).

The Protestant work ethic has its roots in Calvinism, a theological system proposed by a 16th century group of Christian reformers led by John Calvin (1509-1564). Calvinists had attained enlightenment by breaking away from the traditional views held by the Catholic Church and instead embraced scientific advancements and intellectual discourse. Before Calvinism, working hard was believed to be only for the poor. Catholics, in general, discouraged hard work and the accumulation of wealth. Calvinism, however, changed the perceptions that Christians had held toward work. Calvinists believed that God demanded that humans live constructive lives of hard work and that laziness would invariably lead them on the path to sinning. Calvinists thus urged Christians to work hard, to be diligent, and to stop wasting time. The accumulation of wealth was seen as a positive, and poverty was seen as undesirable. In the eyes of Calvinists, physical work was a calling from God, and all human beings were created to work in the service of God. Calvinists asserted that accumulated wealth should serve the glory of God, such as by making donations to the church, and therefore should not be spent on leisure or other personal enjoyment purposes. Life, in their view, was meant to be all work and no play. Calvinism became a natural catalyst for the coming Industrial Revolution. Max Weber found that the well-developed capitalist-based societies of northern Europe created by the Industrial Revolution were dominated by Protestant populations rooted in Calvinist thought. These societies stood in contrast with the Catholic-dominated societies of southern Europe, which included Italy and Spain. His findings led him to coin the phrase "Protestant work ethic."

Making Inferences

Check (✓) the statements you think a Calvinist would agree with.

1. People should capitalize on every opportunity to make money and to create wealth. ☐

2. Faith and tradition are preferred to reasoning power and scientific achievement. ☐

3. The Protestant work ethic rewards those who practice it with improved living conditions. ☐

4. The rich and members of the clergy should not engage in hard, physical work. ☐

5. If people accumulate wealth, they can spend it on living a relaxed, enjoyable lifestyle. ☐

Reflections   The Protestant work ethic was essential to the creation of the spirit of capitalism. Capitalism, however, distanced itself from religion as it took root around the world. In our time, religion is viewed as a hindrance to the advancement of capitalism. Today's capitalists are largely indifferent to religion, with some even being hostile toward it. Is it possible for capitalism to work again in the service of religion? How so?

The Role-Players of Fantasy

Unit Preview

A. Discuss the following questions.

1. Are you a fan of comic books, computer games, or fantasy movies? Do you own any memorabilia connected to these fiction genres, such as clothing with imprinted images or action figures?

2. Have you ever worn a costume, such as a Halloween costume? If so, what costume was it, and how did it make you feel? If you answered yes to the first question, have you or would you consider wearing a costume of your favorite character from a comic book, computer game, or fantasy movie?

B. Write definitions in English for the following words and expressions. Check your definitions again after reading the passage to make sure they fit the context of the passage.

1. fandom (*n.*) _____

2. practitioner (*n.*) _____

3. legion (*n.*) _____

4. emulate (*v.*) _____

5. don (*v.*) _____

6. masquerade ball (*n.*) _____

7. cross-dress (*v.*) _____

8. communal (*adj.*) _____

9. rendition (*n.*) _____

10. fluttering heart (*idiom*) _____

C. Test your knowledge on the topic of cosplay by checking Yes/No in the table below. After reading the passage, check whether your answers were correct or not.

Background Knowledge	True?	
	Yes	No
1. Dressing up as one's favorite pop star is called cosplay or pop-play.		
2. Cosplay was started in Japan by fans of characters from manga books.		
3. Cosplay increases one's levels of self-confidence.		

It has been described as a hobby, an expression of fandom appreciation, and a performance art form. To some, it is a profession and even a way of life. It is studied in art departments in universities and celebrated at hugely popular comic and anime conventions. Its practice empowers one's creativity and increases the confidence of its practitioners in their bodies and physical abilities. This cultural phenomenon that derives its name—cosplay—from the words "costume" and "role-play" involves the transformation of legions of anime, manga, video game, movie, and history buffs into the fictional and historical characters they emulate.

Cosplayers or players, as they are more simply referred to, can assemble in a wondrous Awase Cosplay—a group of players who dress up according to a similar theme—or make individual appearances dressed as characters from manga series such as *Neon Genesis Evangelion*, *Dragon Ball*, or *Rozen Maiden*, video games such as *Tekken 6*, comic book heroes such as Spider-Man or Wonder Woman, characters from TV series such as *Game of Thrones*, and even historical figures such as Joan of Arc or Emperor Commodus. No matter whose persona and clothes they don, cosplayers are freed from their personal realities and transformed into living performance art pieces.

Spider-man, a Marvel comic book character

Dressing up in character is not unique to cosplay. The first documented case of dressing up in a costume, known as costuming, took place in 1908, when an American couple from Cincinnati partook in a masquerade ball as Mr. Skygack and Miss Pickles, two Martian characters from a newspaper comic. But costuming became a true pop culture phenomenon with the release of the 1975 musical *The Rocky Horror Picture Show*. Men and women fans of this Gothic musical felt liberated by cross-dressing in skimpy outfits accentuated by blood-red lipstick, fishnets, corsets, top hats, and canes. And then there was the World Science Fiction Convention, where devoted followers of *Star Trek*, *Star Wars*, and other sci-fi movies would jump in a costume of their favorite aliens in a New York minute[1].

It was actually at the 1984 World Sci-fi Convention

What did they mean?

1 Explain the following Harry Winston quote: "People will stare. Make it worth their while."

What did they mean?

2 Explain the following Coco Chanel quote: "In order to be irreplaceable, one must always be different."

Man in a fantasy costume of a dark demon

that Japanese manga reporter and publisher Nobuyuki Takahashi had an aha moment[2] and coined the term cosplay, giving Japanese anime and manga character costuming enthusiasts a better way to describe what they had been doing since the 1970s. Costuming continues to be a central aspect of cultural events such as Halloween and celebrations such as the Carnival, and it has defined a number of music genres, from the British Glam Rock inspired by David Bowie to the Japanese visual *kei* typified by X-Japan.

The term "cosplay" was coined in Japan in 1984.

There is little doubt that cosplayers are huge fans of the characters they portray, but cosplay is much more than fandom. The latter is a communal phenomenon, bringing together enthusiasts through social media or personal interactions during conventions, or cons, as they share information connected to their common fantasies. Cosplay, however, gives fans a way of interacting in a more intimate way. Players can spend hundreds of dollars and countless hours creating their costumes and refining their rendition of a beloved character down to the tiniest detail.

When one becomes a living 3-D version of Wonder Woman, she gives inspiration and courage to everyone in fandom, who cheer her on with broad smiles and fluttering hearts, and perhaps to the little girl who bravely wants to hug her and say, "I want to grow up to be just like you." Moments such as this bring meaning to cosplayers and continue to advance the culture of cosplay to a collective creation of traditions, products, and ideas.

What did they mean?

3 Explain the following Iris Apfel quote: "When you don't dress like everybody else, you don't have to think like everybody else."

→ **IDIOMS: Usage and Etymology** ←

1 in a New York minute: This idiom has the figurative meaning of "something happening very quickly," a reference to New York City's fast-paced life. The idiom may have originated in Texas in the mid-1900s as a comparison of New York's fast-paced life to the slower life in Texas.

2 have an aha moment: The idiom has the figurative meaning of "having a sudden realization or reaching a point when you suddenly understand something." The origin of this idiom can be traced to the German phrase aha-*erlebnis* (a moment of insight), used as early as 1908, and to English use with a similar meaning starting in the 1930s. The idiom gained popularity on the *Oprah Winfrey Show*, where it acquired the meaning of "having an insight into yourself."

Reading Comprehension

Choose the best answers to the following questions on the passage "The Role-Players of Fantasy."

Inference

1. Where in the passage would the following sentence fit best?

"In this sense, cosplay can be thought of as a performance art form."

a. at the beginning of the first paragraph

b. at the end of the second paragraph

c. at the beginning of the fourth paragraph

d. at the end of the last paragraph

Did You Know? ∞∞∞∞∞∞

The word "layer" is the Japanese slang word for cosplayer. Layer Support is a cleaning service designed specifically for cosplay costumes.

Detail

2. Which of the following is NOT a fictional character?

a. Mr. Skygack

b. Emperor Commodus

c. Miss Pickles

d. Wonder Woman

Detail

3. Which of the following statements is true according to the passage?

a. *The Rocky Horror Picture Show* is a Gothic musical involving cross-dressing.

b. An Awase Cosplay is a group of players who make individual appearances.

c. The first documented case of public costuming occurred in 1975.

d. David Bowie was part of the visual *kei* typified by X-Japan.

Vocabulary

4. Which word pair does NOT fit in with the others?

a. cosplayer / convention

b. music fan / concert

c. character / legion

d. participant / carnival

Vocabulary

5. Which of the following words is a synonym of the highlighted word in paragraph 3?

a. imaginative   b. ample   c. revealing   d. elegant

Did You Know? ∞∞∞∞∞∞

Cosplay Is Not Consent is a women's movement that aims to prevent sexual harassment, such as picture-taking without permission, verbal abuse, and the touching or groping of players, at cosplay conventions.

Inference

6. What can be implied from the passage about cosplayers?

a. They are primarily motivated by a desire to make money through cosplay.

b. They wear costumes of their heroes to make up for a lack of creativity.

c. Their confidence levels soar when they put on their costumes.

d. They feel liberated when they return to their normal lives after cosplaying.

Inference

7. Which of the following analogies best describes cosplay?

a. buying a lottery ticket and then winning it and becoming super-rich

b. performing a role in one's high school's year-end drama club production

c. going on a mountaineering expedition and climbing Mount Everest

d. getting hired at one's dream job by the best company in the field

Proofreading and Writing Practice

A. Read the following passages. Find 5 mistakes in each paragraph and correct them.

1. Enako Ring, or Enako Wall, as she is ~~sometime~~ *sometimes* referred to, is Japan's most popular cosplayer. When she makes a private appearance, she commands the attention of the crowds that show up to cheer her on and get a snapshot opportunity. Enako Ring started being the anime characters from *The Melancholy of Haruhi Suzumiya* and *Rozen Maiden* in 2007. She is also a singer and voice actor, and her voice has been used in several Japanese animation productions. It's no wonder that Enako Ring has a huge follower on Twitter.

2. The global market for cosplay products, which includes everything from costumes to makeup, topped 100 billions dollars in 2019. This market has created a variety of job opportunity for professional cosplayers, such as brand ambassadors. Additional sources of debt for professional cosplayers include acting, modeling, clothing design, and appearances on social media. Presence on YouTube, Instagram, and Twitter is almost a must for profession cosplayers. A career in cosplay also has involved constant travel time to cosplay conventions and related events held around the world.

B. Make an argument for or against cosplaying controversial historical figures such as Genghis Khan or Kim Jong-il. Your argument should contain your opinion as well as supporting facts and should be around 150 words.

Vocabulary in Context

A. Complete the conversation below with vocabulary from the passage.

| fandom | cross-dressing | masquerade ball | don |

A: Toby, can I count on seeing you at the _____¹ this weekend?

B: I'll be at the ball for sure. I even bought a mask for the occasion.

A: What are you dressing up as?

B: I think I'll _____² my old Zoro outfit. It always attracts attention.

A: Sure, Zoro still has a huge _____³ around the world. I'm a fan, too.

B: What about you? Are you thinking of trying something different this time?

A: Actually, I'm thinking of doing a bit of _____⁴.

B: Wow, that's bold of you. Your sister's closet should give you some ideas.

B. Choose the sentences where the underlined words have the same meanings as they do in the passage.

1.   a. This 13th-century northern France cathedral is built in the <u>Gothic</u> style.

     b. The poem "The Raven" is a fine example of American <u>Gothic</u> literature.

2.   a. K-pop boy bands and girl bands have <u>legions</u> of fans around the world.

     b. The sight of Roman <u>legions</u> would send barbarians running for the hills.

3.   a. The translation is the book's first <u>rendition</u> in the English language.

     b. The court approved the criminal's <u>rendition</u> to his home country.

C. Complete the chart below with definitions for the given phrases using "grow." Then, write sentences using the phrases.

Phrases	Definitions
1. grow up	*to act in a mature way and not childishly*
2. grow apart	
3. doesn't grow on trees	
4. grow cold	
5. hear the grass grow	

1. *You always joke around when we have work to do.* **Grow up** *already and give us a hand!*

2. _____

3. _____

4. _____

5. _____

Reading Connections

Read the following passage on comic books and manga. Then, do the exercises.

Comic Books and Manga:
The 2D Universes That Inspire Cosplay

🎧 04

Comic books provide Hollywood the source material for blockbuster movie franchises such as *Batman*, *Spider-Man*, and *The Avengers* though they are not widely read by Americans. In contrast, Japanese comic books, known as manga, have a large Japanese readership that reaches across all demographics; it includes young men and women as well as adults. The stories of the superheroes depicted in comic books and their *shonen* counterparts in manga continue to inspire and sustain the practice of cosplay in the U.S. and Japan and throughout the world. As one might expect, the 2D universes of comic books and manga have unique and distinct sets of characteristics.

Comic books and manga are literally read differently. Comic books are read from left to right while manga are read from right to left. This includes word balloons and text boxes. Comic book readers will also notice that manga lacks color and sometimes detail in its drawings. Comic books are generally colored and depict a high level of realism in their drawings.

In the superhero comic universe, alliances, in-fighting, and full-scale wars between various groups and factions are the norm. While manga has its share of drama, themes based on friendship and collaboration are more commonly explored and valued. Manga characters such as Goku and Sailor Moon look and feel different from their caped superhero counterparts in comic books. Unlike superheroes, who remain largely unchanged, the *shonen* continue to develop and grow their powers. Keeping this in mind, one would be justified to argue that Goku is—or will be—more powerful than Superman.

A story must always arrive to an end. Or must it? Comic books are open-ended, meaning that Batman will never stop fighting crime; only the villains and the nature of the fights will change over time. In manga, the story plots have a beginning and a lengthy middle but also an eventual ending. In the manga universe, there is no such thing as a reboot.

Making Inferences
Check (✓) the statements you think the author of the above passage would agree with.

1. The drawings in manga books look and feel more realistic than the ones in comic books. ☐

2. American comic book readers can easily adapt to reading manga stories. ☐

3. The story of Sailor Moon has to come to an eventual ending. ☐

4. Superman's struggle against the forces of evil is eternal; only the villains will change. ☐

5. Hollywood can probably benefit more from manga heroes than from comic book ones. ☐

Reflections American actress Scarlett Johansson was cast in the role of Major Kusanagi in the 2017 movie *Ghost in the Shell*. The movie is based on the Japanese manga by the same name, and for this reason, many manga fans across Japan and Asia were hoping to see a Japanese woman cast in this role. Should movies based on comic books and manga characters be culture specific, or is it okay that actors from different ethnicities portray these characters?

The Perils of Travel to the

d Planet

Unit Preview

A. Discuss the following questions.

1. What agency is in charge of your country's space program? What are some of its plans for the future exploration of space?

2. Has a man or woman from your country ever flown into space? Who and when?

B. Write definitions in English for the following words and expressions. Check your definitions again after reading the passage to make sure they fit the context of the passage.

1. void (*n.*)

2. daunting (*adj.*)

3. dispatch (*v.*)

4. tackle (*v.*)

5. kink (*n.*)

6. wreak havoc on (*phr.*)

7. cataract (*n.*)

8. morale (*n.*)

9. double as (*phr.*)

10. indicative (*adj.*)

C. Test your knowledge on the topic of space travel by checking Yes/No in the table below. After reading the passage, check whether your answers were correct or not.

Background Knowledge	True?	
	Yes	No
1. A few countries have already flown spacecraft to Mars.		
2. The biggest obstacle to living on Mars is the lack of air.		
3. Mars has a similar gravity field to that found on Earth.		

Artist's rendition of a space station in orbit around Mars

What did they mean? 10

1 Explain the following Martin Luther King, Jr. quote: "Only in the darkness can you see the stars." 15

What did they mean?

2 Explain the following William Shakespeare quote: "It is not in the stars to hold our destiny, but in ourselves." 30

A voyage to Mars, based on current space flight technology, would take anywhere from five to ten months. During that time, if all goes well, a spaceship will hurl itself through the 482 million kilometers of cosmic void at speeds of up to 21,000 kilometers an hour. But that "if" may seem like pie in the sky[1], especially when you throw humans into the equation. The perils associated with flying humans to the Red Planet are daunting, and to make this dream a reality, humanity's brightest minds are already hard at work on this out-of-this-world task.

Robotic spacecraft have already been dispatched to Mars in flyby missions, where spacecraft would fly past Mars; orbiting missions, where spacecraft would orbit Mars; landing missions, where spacecraft would land on the surface of the planet; and rover missions, where spacecraft landing on Mars would deploy robotic explorers that would then get around and inspect the surface of the planet.

So far, only the U.S. has been able to complete all of these types of missions. Russia has managed to complete flybys and orbiting and landing missions but has not been able to deploy a rover yet, while the EU and India have only been able to place spacecraft in orbit around Mars. Of the 56 missions sent to Mars, only 26 have been successful, a ratio that highlights the first problem with flying to Mars: the reliability of the available spaceship technology. Before sending astronauts on their way to the Red Planet, we need to tackle with confidence the challenges of building reliable spaceships.

Supposing that engineers do work out the mind-boggling kinks in spaceship design, the truly difficult challenges emerge. Of these, none is greater than space radiation. Humans were made to live on the Earth, whose magnetic field and atmosphere combine to block dangerous particles such as energetic protons produced by the sun's activity and the far deadlier galactic cosmic radiation produced by distant supernova explosions. These invisible killers that travel at almost the speed at light would wreak havoc on the human body traveling through space, with effects ranging from eye cataracts to genetic mutations, cancer, and even strokes. Astronauts will somehow need to be shielded from space radiation.

On a return journey to Mars, astronauts will also need to move between three different gravity fields: the Earth's gravity field; the weightlessness encountered during the six-month journey through deep space; and Mars' gravity field, which is three-eighths as strong as the Earth's. Gravity changes have a profound effect on one's hand-eye coordination, balance, movement, and sense of space and affect the muscles, heart, and bones. To put this in context, in weightlessness, an astronaut's bone density will drop by one percent each month.

Humans are a social species of beings. Isolation during a long journey through space can feel like a month of Sundays[2] and lead to a decline in mood, cognition, morale, and interpersonal interactions. These conditions can develop into mental or physical illness, both of which are quite undesirable in space. The packaging, preservation, and proper administration of medicine in space is easier said than done. Astronauts will have to double as doctors and psychologists in conditions that defy our understanding of medicine.

James Lovell, one of the first NASA astronauts to fly around the Moon, made a beautifully paradoxical observation about space flight: "The real friends of the space voyager are the stars. Their friendly, familiar patterns are constant companions, unchanging, out there." That a source of deadly cosmic radiation would become a space voyager's trusted friend is indicative of the perils of reaching the Red Planet. And Lovell would know a thing or two about it.

35

40

50

55

What did they mean?

3 Explain the following Robert Breault quote: "Metaphor for the night sky: a trillion asterisks and no explanations."

The actual color of Mars is a dull gray, as seen in this black-and-white picture—the red color is seen only when light hits dust storms on the planet's surface.

IDIOMS: Usage and Etymology

1 **pie in the sky:** The idiom has the meaning of "something that is unrealistic or cannot be achieved." The idiom comes from the early 20th-century song "The Preacher and the Slave," written by Joe Hill, a radical labor union organizer. The song and the phrase parodied the promise of salvation in the afterlife as something pleasant to imagine but realistically unattainable.

2 **a month of Sundays:** The idiom has the figurative meaning of "a long time or many months" and the literal meaning of 30-31 weeks, which is the amount of time it takes a "month of Sundays" to pass. The idiom originates from the Christian holy day of Sunday, the Sabbath, a long day of rest without fun.

Reading Comprehension

Inference

1. **Where in the passage would the following sentence fit best?**

   "In short, space is not the friendliest environment for the human body."

   a. at the beginning of the last paragraph

   b. at the end of the last paragraph

   c. at the end of the fifth paragraph

   d. at the beginning of the sixth paragraph

Did You Know? ◇◇◇◇◇◇◇◇◇◇

Zero gravity can decrease the size of one's love. Well... metaphorically speaking, that is. In scientific terms, humans lose muscle mass in space, so their hearts actually shrink. Smaller hearts, smaller love?

Detail

2. **Which of the following can be an astronaut's best and worst friends?**

   a. stars   b. weightlessness   c. robotic explorers   d. medicine

Detail

3. **Which of the following statements is true according to the passage?**

   a. The U.S. and Russia have placed robotic explorers on the surface of Mars.

   b. A number of countries have sent reliable spaceships to Mars.

   c. Mental and physical illnesses are quite impossible to have in space.

   d. Astronauts will have to move through three types of gravitational fields to reach Mars.

Vocabulary

4. **Which word pair does NOT fit in with the others?**

   a. rover / explorer   b. supernova / void

   c. isolation / interaction   d. dream / reality

Vocabulary

5. **Which of the following is synonymous with the highlighted phrase in paragraph 1?**

   a. disregard humans   b. consider humans

   c. solve humans   d. ask humans

Did You Know? ◇◇◇◇◇◇◇◇◇◇

Mars has two moons: Phobos and Deimos. Both are much smaller than Earth's Moon. Phobos is 22km in diameter, and Deimos is 13km in diameter, and they have elongated shapes, which make them resemble asteroids.

Inference

6. **What can be inferred from Lovell's reference to the stars as "constant, unchanging companions"?**

   a. The stars are beautiful as well as paradoxical celestial bodies.

   b. The stars are always friendly toward space voyagers.

   c. The stars are an accurate indication of the perils of travel to the Red Planet.

   d. The known and familiar can feel reassuring to space travelers.

Inference

7. **Which of the following quotes best sums up the perils of space travel?**

   a. "Writing is a journey into the unknown." (Charlie Kaufman)

   b. "The world is so dangerous a man is lucky to get out of it alive." (W.C. Fields)

   c. "The fishermen know that the sea is dangerous, but they have never found this sufficient reason for remaining ashore." (Vincent van Gogh)

   d. "Life is weird, great, and dangerous." (Henry Rollins)

Proofreading and Writing Practice

A. Read the following passages. Find 5 mistakes in each paragraph and correct them.

essential

1. Personality characteristics are ~~essentially~~ in group interactions. A well-functioning group must have a leader, a mixture of personalities such as introverts and extraverts, and also a clown. The humor provided by the clown can defuse the tensions that occur naturally during long periods of close contact, such as during spaced travel or living in a colony on Mars. The clown also acts as a bridge between different groups of people, such as the astronauts in a spaceship and the ground control crew up on the Earth. Researchers have found that groups that lack clowns tend to experience in-fighting or lose co-herence.

2. In the movie *The Martian*, actor Matt Damon is seen knock down by a violent dust storm on Mars. In reality, the dust storms on Mars are not as gentle as portrayed in the movie mainly because the air on Mars is only one percent as dense as the air on the Earth. Due to this thinly air, dust storms can form rather quickly on Mars, but the wind generated by them would feel like a gentle summer breeze on the Earth. However, because the Martian air is so rare, it takes a long time—days and even weeks—for the dust to finally settle back on the surface of the sun. This makes Martian rain storms quite problematic since solar power generation can be interrupted for long periods of time.

B. Make an argument for the need to establish human colonies on distant planets. Your argument should contain your opinion as well as supporting facts and should be around 150 words.

Vocabulary in Context

cataract	dispatched	morale	double as	wreak havoc

A: Mom, I'm just calling to make sure you know about the coming hurricane.

B: Yes, I've heard. The city has _____¹ police officers to knock on doors to inform everyone about it. But thanks for calling, sweetie.

A: They said that the strong winds will _____² on gardens and trees. There will be flooding, too.

B: I know. My neighbors are all jittery. _____³ is very low around the neighborhood right now. Everyone is expecting the worst.

A: Do you have everything you need?

B: I've done my shopping, but now I have to _____⁴ a babysitter for your sister's cats. She's gone on vacation and left them with me.

A: Well, the good thing is they'll keep you company during the storm.

B: True. But you know, Mitty, the yellow one, has a _____⁵ in her left eye. I'll have to take her to the vet after the hurricane passes.

Did You Know?

Mars is currently populated by robots—human-made landers and rovers, that is. Three of them are Russian built and nonoperational, one is British and nonoperational, one is European and nonoperational, and 10 are American, two of which are operational: Curiosity and InSight.

B. Choose the sentences where the underlined words have the same meanings as they do in the passage.

1. a. The death of her pet turtle left a great void in Gwyneth's life.

  b. The diver stared over the edge of the coral reef and into the void below.

2. a. Marco felt a kink in his neck from sleeping in an awkward position.

  b. Nico had to fix the kink in the program before the system crashed again.

3. a. The company tackled the issue of internal theft by increasing security.

  b. The center-back tackled the opposing striker to save a last-minute goal.

C. Complete the chart below with definitions for the given phrases using "get." Then, write sentences using the phrases.

Phrases	Definitions
1. get around	*to have mobility*
2. get back at	
3. get around to	
4. get something across	
5. get over something	

Did You Know?

The famous "Face on Mars" is similar to a *mesa*—a land mass found in the deserts of the American West. Due to light and shadow effects, this Martian rock formation looks almost human.

1. *My sister prefers **getting around** by car; I prefer public transportation.*

2. _____

3. _____

4. _____

5. _____

Read the following passage on the establishment of a human base on Mars. Then, do the exercises.

Living on MARS

🎧 06

The idea of establishing a human presence on Mars is no longer the subject of science fiction; plans for it are now being drawn up by NASA and even private space companies such as SpaceX. But establishing a human base on Mars makes the task of getting there seem trivial by comparison. Despite its serene image when peered through a telescope, the Martian environment is grimly inhospitable.

For starters, the weather on Mars is so cold that even adjectives like bone-chilling don't do it justice. The average temperature on Mars is -60 degrees Celsius, with temperatures ranging from -126 to -20 degrees Celsius, depending on the location and the time of the year. The temperatures can fluctuate dramatically even during a single week. And it is not like one could just call up NASA and ask someone there to send over more blankets. The call alone would take about 15 minutes to reach the Earth...

The gravity on Mars is about 38 percent that of the Earth's, so walking would take a bit of getting used to. With a nimble and sturdy Mars rover, however, astronauts could visit places such as Olympus Mons—the tallest volcano in the solar system, rising 25,000 meters above its surrounding plains—or journey to Mars's polar ice caps, where dry ice snowfall happens on occasion. Leaving their shielded base, however, would expose astronauts to deadly cosmic radiation. But staying put inside the base would also not be without problems.

NASA has found that being away from Earth on long-duration space missions can have unpredictable effects on groups of people. In 1973, for example, three astronauts aboard the first American space station, Skylab, basically went on strike and stopped doing their tasks for a period of time. Group dynamics, the stress of being in space, and other factors were given as reasons for the work disruption, but ultimately it all comes down to a simple and undeniable fact: space is lonely and unforgiving, and being far from home is awfully unnatural for any human being.

Making Inferences

Check (✓) the statements you think an astronaut living on Mars would agree with.

1. Mars lacks any interesting geographical features worth exploring. ☐

2. Communication with the Earth would hardly be a problem for Martian colonists. ☐

3. Disagreements between Martian colonists would not be inconceivable. ☐

4. Due to the freezing temperatures, Martian colonists would frequently see snowfall. ☐

5. Being on Mars would feel unnatural for most colonists despite the planet's beauty. ☐

Reflections   Earth has a limited lifespan. It was born from solar activity and will eventually die in a fiery death, engulfed by the sun's final explosion. If our species survives that long, humans will need to find a new home. Should we start "home-shopping" now while there is no immediate danger to our planet, or should we delay the search for a new home until we have a clear reason to do so?

UFOs: Everything We Don't Know About Space Travel

Unit Preview

A. Discuss the following questions.

1. Do you believe that UFOs are spaceships that belong to alien species, or do you believe they are secret flying objects created by advanced military programs?

2. Have you ever seen something you could not explain, or have any of your friends or family members mentioned seeing something unexplained? If so, could you describe it?

B. Write definitions in English for the following words and expressions. Check your definitions again after reading the passage to make sure they fit the context of the passage.

1. orbit (*v.*) ....

2. far-fetched (*adj.*) ....

3. resounding (*adj.*) ....

4. intricacies (*n.*) ....

5. abduct (*v.*) ....

6. fabrication (*n.*) ....

7. optics (*n.*) ....

8. intercept (*v.*) ....

9. hypersonic (*adj.*) ....

10. maneuver (*n.*) ....

C. Test your knowledge on the topic of UFOs by checking Yes/No in the table below. After reading the passage, check whether your answers were correct or not.

Background Knowledge	True?	
	Yes	No
1. There are over a trillion galaxies like the Milky Way in the universe.		
2. People have been photographing UFOs since the 19th century.		
3. In 2020, humans established contact with an alien species.		

If they do indeed exist and are of alien origin, it stands to reason that unidentified flying objects (UFOs) are capable of space travel. To some people, the very possibility of their existence is simply terrifying. To others, as sci-fi writer Arthur C. Clarke smartly pointed out, the possibility that we could be alone in the universe is equally terrifying.

UFO sightings have been documented for over 100 years.

The numbers suggest that we are not alone. NASA has estimated that in our galaxy, at least 20 percent of the approximately 200 billion existing stars are likely orbited by a rocky planet classified as potentially habitable. It wouldn't be far-fetched to find that one of those rocks, like our planet, can support carbon-based life. And that's just in our galaxy. Multiply that by some two trillion galaxies that exist in our known universe, and the odds will go up impressively. And that's not all, if we accept the existence of parallel universes.

But if there is life out there other than on the Earth, would those life forms be capable of space travel? The evidence points to a resounding yes. After all, humans have done it. Sure, it took *Homo sapiens* some 200,000 years to figure out the intricacies of space flight, but having done it ourselves, chances are that other life forms will have figured it out, too. Some will surely have been able to do it a lot better than we can. And there is reason to believe that such a scenario is not strictly theoretical.

UFO sightings, whether real or imagined, have been documented for over 100 years, with the first photographs of a UFO taken in 1883 by Mexican astronomer Jose Bonilla. In 2019, there were some 6,000 UFO sightings in the U.S. alone, with tens of thousands more in countries around the world. And people do not just keep seeing UFOs; millions actually claimed to have been abducted and released by alien spaceships. The vast majority of these claims should be taken with a pinch of salt[1], however, and

Is there life out there other than on Earth?

What did they mean?

1 Explain the following Yogi Berra quote: "If you don't know where you're going, you'll probably end up somewhere else."

What did they mean?

2 Explain the following Carl Sagan quote: "If a human disagrees with you, let him live. In a hundred billion galaxies, you will not find another."

indeed, scientists have **brushed aside** most claims with reasons ranging from dirty camera lenses to fabrications of the human mind due to its desire to find stability in a confused world.

UFOs in ancient Egyptian frescoes

Those types of explanations may hold for people who have taken snapshots of UFOs on their mobile phones or seen flying saucers after having one beer too many in a bar. But when such sightings are reported by the world's best-trained fighter pilots flying in machines equipped with the most advanced optics ever produced by mankind, we are hopelessly and collectively left scratching our heads[2].

After all, what can be said of a November 23, 1953 incident, when First Lieutenant Felix Eugene Moncla, Jr.'s plane vanished out of the Michigan sky, never to be found, after being sent to intercept a UFO? And how can anyone explain away a video of a UFO shot by Navy Fighter Squadron Commander David Fravor using his F/A-18 Super Hornet's high-tech infrared tracking system?

There is just too much we do not know about space travel. Commander Fravor's jet fighter, flying off the aircraft carrier USS Nimitz, recorded video of a UFO that defies our understanding of the physics of flight: hypersonic speeds, instantaneous stops, impossible acceleration, and instantaneous changes of direction. If flying machines that can produce such astounding flight maneuvers and travel at such speeds are real, they must be the product of a superior intelligence that must know everything we do not know about space travel. For us, for now, those unknowns remain a universe of possibilities.

45

What did they mean?

3 Explain the following Konstantin Tsiolkovsky quote: "Earth is the cradle of humanity, but one cannot live in a cradle forever."

50

55

→ **IDIOMS:** Usage and Etymology ←

1 **take with a pinch/grain of salt:** This idiom has the figurative meaning of "viewing something with skepticism or not interpreting something literally." The idiom originated in ancient Greece in 77 A.D. when Pliny the Elder translated an ancient antidote for poison that recommended taking the antidote with a "grain of salt." The current usage of the idiom has been around since the mid-1900s.

2 **scratch one's head:** This idiom has the figurative meaning of "expressing puzzlement or uncertainty." The origin of the idiom may be found in the literal gesture of scratching one's head when contemplating something puzzling.

Reading Comprehension

Choose the best answers to the following questions on the passage "UFOs: Everything We Don't Know About Space Travel."

Inference

1. Where in the passage would the following phrase fit best?

"That is, its intent to make sense of a world that is filled with uncertainty."

a. at the end of the first paragraph

b. at the end of the second paragraph

c. at the end of the fourth paragraph

d. at the end of the last paragraph

Did You Know? ∞∞∞∞∞∞∞∞∞

The Apollo 11 astronauts left a plaque on the Moon with the following inscription: "Here men from the planet Earth first set foot upon the Moon July 1969, A.D. We came in peace for all mankind."

Detail

2. Which of the following men did not witness a UFO incident?

a. Arthur C. Clarke

b. Jose Bonilla

c. Felix Eugene Moncla

d. David Fravor

Did You Know? ∞∞∞∞∞∞∞∞∞

The Foo Fighters, the name of the popular grunge/alternative rock band from Seattle, got its name from a term used by Allied pilots during World War 2 to describe UFOs and other mysterious aerial phenomena.

Detail

3. Which of the following statements is true according to the passage?

a. UFO sightings are a uniquely 20th-century phenomenon.

b. High-tech equipment on fighter planes cannot track UFOs.

c. Other planets in our galaxy cannot support carbon-based life.

d. Some pictures of UFOs may be the results of dirty camera lenses.

Vocabulary

4. Which word pair does NOT fit in with the others?

a. mobile phones / snapshots

b. fighter planes / maneuvers

c. spaceships / travel

d. aircraft carriers / machines

Vocabulary

5. Which of the following words is an antonym of the highlighted phrase in paragraph 4?

a. ignored   b. accepted   c. challenged   d. dismissed

Inference

6. Which of the following statements echoes Arthur C. Clarke's comment in paragraph 1?

a. Living in isolation is a desirable proposition.

b. The existence of UFOs is often met with ambivalence.

c. It is considered ideal not to know your neighbors.

d. Space travel can eliminate all human fears and anxieties.

Inference

7. Which of the following best relates to the theme of this passage?

a. "The human failing I would most like to correct is aggression." (Stephen Hawking)

b. "Space is only an hour's drive away if your car could go upwards." (Fred Hoyle)

c. "Astronomy taught us our insignificance in Nature." (Ralph Waldo Emerson)

d. "I look up at the stars and wonder, how self-important are we to think that we are the only life-form?" (Katy Perry)

Proofreading and Writing Practice

A. Read the following passages. Find 5 mistakes in each paragraph and correct them.

1. UFOs were initially referred ~~toward~~ *to* as flying saucers, a term coined in 1947 by pilot Kenneth Arnold. Donald

   E. Keyhoe's 1953 book, *Flying Saucers from Outer Space,* was the first books to use the term UFO. The U.S.

   Air Force adopted the term UFO in 1953 in order to include shapes others than saucers (discs). Project Blue

   Book, a UFO research agency belonging to the U.S. Air Force, cataloged some 12,618 UFO sightings between

   1947 and 1969, with 701 of them remaining to this day unidentified. UFOs that are later unidentified as an

   object of Earthly origin can be called identified flying objects.

2. A UFO religion advocates the existence of extrarestrial beings that travel by using UFOs. Two noteble examples

   of UFO religions are the Aetherius Society and the Church of Scientology. Scientology was founded by L.

   Ron Hubbard in 1952 while the Aetherius Society was funded by George King in 1954. King claimed to

   have received a command from interplanetary sources to become "the Voice of Interplanetary Parliament."

   Hubbard, meanwhile, started his religious colt as a "spiritual healing technology." These religions have attracted

   thousands—and in some cases millions—of followings throughout the world, including celebrities. Tom Cruise

   is a well-known Scientologist.

B. Make an argument for the benefit(s) of establishing contact with another intelligent species of beings living in our universe. Your argument should contain your opinion as well as supporting facts and should be around 150 words.

Vocabulary in Context

A. Complete the conversation below with vocabulary from the passage.

far-fetched   abducted   hypersonic   intricacies   orbiting

A: What's wrong with Matt? He doesn't seem all right lately.

B: It's weird... He keeps saying that his pet iguana was ....[1] by aliens.

A: What? Has he lost his mind? What kind of aliens? And what would they want with his iguana?

B: You know, like ET. I know it sounds ....[2].

A: Nah, it sounds perfectly normal. They must've been ....[3] the Earth in their spaceship when they saw Matt's iguana and thought, "There's our lunch!"

B: But seriously, don't joke around with him. He's very distressed right now.

A: The ....[4] of the human imagination never cease to amaze me!

B: That's our Matt; his imagination is always flying in ....[5] mode.

B. Choose the sentences where the underlined words have the same meanings as they do in the passage.

1. a. The government seems to be unconcerned with the optics of its failed policies.

   b. The camera body is fine, but the optics are not in the best condition.

2. a. The fabrication of ship and submarine propellers is a tough skill to master.

   b. The story printed in the newspaper is a complete fabrication.

3. a. The F-35 stealth plane pulled off some impressive maneuvers at the air show.

   b. The U.S. and Korea have postponed military maneuvers for the time being.

C. Complete the chart below with definitions for the given phrases using "come." Then, write sentences using the phrases.

Phrases	Definitions
1. come about	to happen, sometimes by chance
2. come into	
3. come through	
4. come under	
5. come up against	

1. *The success of Glynn's restaurant **came about** after a couple of previous failed attempts.*

2. ....

3. ....

4. ....

5. ....

Read the following passage on this decade's calendar for space travel. Then, do the exercises.

Space Travel Calendar 2020-2030 🎧 08

The past decade was relatively busy in terms of space exploration. Notable space observations included earthquakes on Mars, detailed views of Pluto, and the first-ever photographs of a black hole. In terms of space flight, a Japanese probe was able to reach and closely observe an asteroid zipping through our solar system while various spacecraft were sent to explore or land on the Moon and Mars. The space exploration calendar for the coming decade is even more jam-packed with exciting missions in the area of space travel.

In the beginning of 2021, NASA plans to land a new rover on Mars, which is scheduled to explore the planet for a whole Mars year (687 Earth days). In 2021, NASA also plans to launch the James Webb Space Telescope, a much-improved successor to the Hubble Space Telescope, and hopes to peer deep into the mysteries of the formation of the early universe. In 2022, the European Space Agency (ESA) will launch an orbiter telescope dubbed Euclid to study dark matter, which makes up 95 percent of the universe but whose understanding remains as elusive as its name. The following year, NASA plans to launch a spacecraft that will study Europa—Jupiter's fourth-largest moon—in an effort to discover whether this icy body can sustain life. In 2024, NASA has plans to return to the Moon in style by landing the first woman astronaut there. The lunar mission will focus on learning how to live and operate on the surface of a celestial body in preparation for a possible flight to Mars. In 2025, the Japan Aerospace Exploration Agency (JAXA) intends to launch a spacecraft that will explore Phobos and Deimos, the two moons of Mars, with the aim of collecting and returning samples from one of these moons back to the Earth. In 2026, NASA will land an octocopter drone named Dragonfly on Titan, the largest of Saturn's 82 moons. Its mission will be to find out whether Titan's environment is habitable. Titan is the only celestial body in our solar system that has an atmosphere with a similar pressure to the Earth's atmosphere. Finally, there is the much-anticipated NASA mission to Mars, with plans that call for humans to orbit or possibly land on Mars in the early 2030s. It will be a busy decade indeed.

Making Inferences

Check (✓) the statements you think a NASA scientist would agree with.

1. The past decade represented an all-time low for humanity in terms of space exploration. ☐

2. Black hole photographs give scientists important clues about how the universe works. ☐

3. In the next decade, powerful new telescopes will help increase our understanding of the universe. ☐

4. NASA's mission to Mars calls for the establishment of a human colony on the Red Planet. ☐

5. Titan may provide proof that planets with similar atmospheric conditions to the Earth's do exist. ☐

Reflections   Despite having existed for hundreds of thousands of years, humanity is in its infancy in terms of understanding the world around it. In a sense, we have just opened our eyes to the stars we see above us. In order to truly understand the universe, we must experience it; we must travel to its infinite destinations. What do you think the chances that you will one day wave goodbye to your grandchildren as they embark on a spaceship to a space camp on a planet in a neighboring galaxy are?

Stan Lee and the Rise of the Marvel Universe

Unit Preview

A. Discuss the following questions.

1. Who is your favorite Marvel character? What about your favorite Marvel movie?

2. Do you know where your favorite Marvel character first appeared? Do you know the person who created this character?

B. Write definitions in English for the following words and expressions. Check your definitions again after reading the passage to make sure they fit the context of the passage.

1. ardent (*adj.*) ....

2. coat of arms (*phr.*) ....

3. pore over (*phr.*) ....

4. gofer (*n.*) ....

5. pen (*v.*) ....

6. in the mold of (*phr.*) ....

7. well-rounded (*adj.*) ....

8. one-dimensional (*adj.*) ....

9. twilight (years) (*n.*) ....

10. cameo (appearance) (*n.*) ....

C. Test your knowledge on the topic of Stan Lee and the Marvel Universe by checking Yes/No in the table below. After reading the passage, check whether your answers were correct or not.

Background Knowledge	True?	
	Yes	No
1. Stan Lee's most famous creation was Superman.		
2. Stan Lee's first creation was Spider-Man.		
3. DC Comics and Marvel Comics traded places as the world's top comics publisher.		

09

Stan Lee co-created the Fantastic Four with Jack Kirby in 1961.

When Stan Lee (1922-2018) passed away at the age of 95, millions of fans across the world tweeted ardent farewells, many signing off with an obscure Latin word: *Excelsior*! The Latin adjective, meaning "higher," had been popularized by the State of New York in 1778, when it included the word on its coat of arms with the meaning of "reaching ever higher." This aspirational call for higher achievement became a universal exclamation of love as Stan Lee was sent off on November 12, 2018, on his voyage to eternity.

Stan Lee's birth name may be enigmatic even to his fans. He was born Stanley Martin Leiber in Manhattan in a poor family of Jewish-Romanian immigrants. The names of Lee's children, however, need no introduction: the Fantastic Four, Spider-Man, Hulk, Thor, Daredevil, X-Men, Iron Man, and many others who were brought forth into the Marvel Universe by Lee's prolific imagination.

Stan Lee's mind started reaching for excelsior from a young age. He read Mark Twain, Jules Verne, and Shakespeare. He loved Charles Dickens and would even pore over the label on the ketchup bottle as he ate his dinner. As he fell in love with the magic of the words he was devouring, Lee dreamed of one day writing the great American novel. Unfortunately for Lee, his dream never came to pass. Luckily for Marvel, he started writing comic books.

Stanley Martin Leiber started out at Timely Comics— the company's name was later changed to Marvel Comics— at the age of 17 as a gofer and was eventually moved up to writing duties. He penned his first comic title, *Captain America Foils the Traitor's Revenge*, at the age of 19 and signed the book under the pen name Stan Lee. The year was 1941 and Stan Lee

10

15

20

25

30

What did they mean?

1 Explain the following Stan Lee quote (from *Spider-Man*): "With great power comes great responsibility."

What did they mean?

2 Explain the following Stan Lee quote (from *Silver Surfer*): "There is only one who is all powerful, and his greatest weapon is love."

Marvel Comics' team of superheroes, the Avengers

had just been made editor-in-chief at Timely Comics.

Throughout the 1940s and 50s, a period referred to as the Golden Age of Comics, Marvel Comics remained a relatively small publisher compared to heavy hitters[1] such as DC Comics, whose Superman and Batman comic books were selling like hotcakes[2]. But the industry was about to undergo dramatic changes.

By 1961, Stan Lee and his team of talented artists, which included Jack Kirby and Steve Ditko, started populating the Marvel Universe with a brand of superheroes and supervillains created in the mold of ordinary people. "They've got these powers. They do wonderful things. But what are the things that worry them? What are the things that frustrate them?" wondered Lee. "I tried to write a well-rounded character with every character I did rather than just somebody who is extra strong and can beat up the bad guys."

Putting this formula to use, Lee first created the Fantastic Four with Jack Kirby in 1961. Then, he made Spider-Man with Steve Ditko, the Incredible Hulk, the X-Men, and Iron Man all in the next couple of years. By 1972, Lee had scripted the first 114 issues of *Fantastic Four* and the first 100 issues of *The Amazing Spider-Man* and brought to life characters that had, like most people, self-doubts and insecurities, sometimes a sense of humor, and oftentimes character flaws. At a time when comic book characters used to feel like one-dimensional paper sketches, Stan Lee gave rise to a Marvel Universe filled with "real flesh-and-blood characters with personality," as he described them.

Stan Lee lived out his twilight years in Hollywood, where he often stepped inside his own fantasies, making cameo appearances in some 35 Marvel movies. Mortality finally proved him to be human, but to millions, Stan Lee is still a superhero. *Excelsior*, Stan!

Hulk is one of Marvel Comics' most popular characters.

What did they mean?

3 Explain the following Stan Lee quote: "The greatest superpower is luck."

→ **IDIOMS: Usage and Etymology** ←

1 **heavy hitter:** This idiom has the figurative meaning of "a greatly successful and influential person." The idiom originated in the sport of boxing, where it was used in its literal sense for a boxer who hit hard. Later, it was also used in baseball, and by the mid-1900s, it started being used in its figurative sense.

2 **selling like hotcakes:** This idiom has the figurative meaning of "selling quickly and in large quantities." The idiom originated in the 19th century, when the term hotcake was coined in American English, meaning "pancake." Pancakes were hot-selling snacks at fairs and festivals, leading to the expression "selling like hotcakes."

Reading Comprehension

Choose the best answers to the following questions on the passage "Stan Lee and the Rise of the Marvel Universe."

Inference

1. Where in the passage would the following sentence fit best?

"At the forefront of these transformations would be Stan Lee and his new brand of superheroes."

a. at the beginning of the fourth paragraph

b. at the beginning of the seventh paragraph

c. at the end of the fifth paragraph

d. at the end of the sixth paragraph

Did You Know? ∞∞∞∞∞∞∞∞

From 1965 until 2001, Stan Lee published a monthly column called *Stan's Soapbox* on the back of each Marvel comic book, which he signed with his favorite catchphrase: "*Excelsior!*"

Detail

2. Which of the following is the literal meaning of "excelsior"?

a. farewell   b. love   c. ardent   d. higher

Detail

3. Which of the following statements is true according to the passage?

a. Stanley Martin Lieber was born Stan Lee.

b. Among Stan Lee's creations were Jules Verne and Charles Dickens.

c. Before Stan Lee, comic book characters lacked realistic personalities.

d. Stan Lee created Spider-Man with Jack Kirby and Steve Ditko.

Did You Know? ∞∞∞∞∞∞∞∞

Stan Lee did not intend for Iron Man to be a popular character: "I thought it would be fun to take the kind of character that nobody would like... and shove it down their throats and make them like him."

Vocabulary

4. Which word pair does NOT fit in with the others?

a. mysterious / baffling

b. perplexing / lucid

c. cryptic / explicit

d. obscure / irrefutable

Vocabulary

5. Which of the following is synonymous with the highlighted phrase in paragraph 3?

a. left intact   b. left alone   c. stood in place   d. took place

Inference

6. Why were Stan Lee's characters an instant hit with large audiences?

a. They had catchy names like Hulk, Spider-Man, and Iron Man.

b. They were perfect one-dimensional paper sketches.

c. They were extra-strong and could beat up the bad guys.

d. They had common traits such as insecurities, doubts, and flaws.

Inference

7. Which of the following superhero quotes best defines Stan Lee?

a. "Heroes are made by the path they choose, not the powers they are graced with." (Iron Man)

b. "With great power comes great responsibility." (Uncle Ben – *Spider-Man*)

c. "Why do we fall? So we can learn to pick ourselves back up." (Batman)

d. "If there's nothing but what we make in this world... let us make it good!" (Beta Ray Bill)

Proofreading and Writing Practice

A. Read the following passages. Find 5 mistakes in each paragraph and correct them.

1. Between 1961, the time he created his first ~~comics~~ *comic* book characters, and 1972, when he moved to Hollywood, Stan Lee wrote at a furious pace: some five books a week. Thanks to Lee's prodigious writing efforts and the invaluable help of his team of artists, Marvel decreased its sales from 18.7 million titles in 1961 to 32 million titles in 1965. The popularity of Stan Lee's creations and the never-growing list of titles in print allowed Marvel to replace DC Comics as the top comic book publisher in the world. Marvel saw its fortunes come to an almost complete collapse in 1996, when it flied for bankruptcy. Marvel eventually got outside of bankruptcy and back into profit, only to be purchased by the Walt Disney Company for 4.3 billion dollars in 2014.

2. At the time of his death, Stan Lee's worthiness was estimated to be between 50 and 80 million dollars. That may sound like a lot of money, but when you consider that the Marvel-inspired movies had gross over $24 billion at the box office prior to his death, his worth looks like a drop in the bucket. As he admitted so himself, Lee had not always made the best financial decisions in death. "I was stupid in a business way. I should have been greedier," he advised. Still, it is not bad at all for a man who never went to college and who started his career as an office go-for for eight dollars a week.

B. Make an argument for the positive impact that comic book heroes can have on young people's ethical development. Your argument should contain your opinion as well as supporting facts and should be around 150 words.

Vocabulary in Context

A. Complete the conversation below with vocabulary from the passage.

gofer	coat of arms	twilight years	penned	cameo appearance

A: Wow, Zeta Holiday is now 70. I remember her last concert in 2000...

B: It's hard to believe she's now in her _____ [1].

A: Didn't she make a voiceover _____ [2] in a Disney movie?

B: I'm not sure. But I know she _____ [3] a cookbook.

A: Really? Have you read it?

B: I just flipped through it at the bookstore. Did you know she started out as a _____ [4] for an insurance company?

A: No kidding. An errand girl?

B: Yup, and now she's famous enough to have her own _____ [5]!

A: She probably does have one with a motto and everything.

B. Choose the sentences where the underlined words have the same meanings as they do in the passage.

1.
 a. Yesterday, I met some ardent fans of martial arts.

 b. The Milky Way Galaxy contains billions of ardent suns.

2.
 a. Our university offers a variety of well-rounded educational programs.

 b. I am happy to see that young Roy developed into a well-rounded adult.

3.
 a. I fail to see how Jeff's personality can be more than one-dimensional.

 b. A shark is a one-dimensional machine meant solely to kill its prey.

Did You Know? ◇◇◇◇◇◇◇◇◇◇

Stan Lee developed a unique method for writing comics at Marvel: He first summarized his stories and then let his artists draw them, giving them the freedom to fill in the details. At the end, he added the dialogue boxes.

C. Complete the chart below with definitions for the given phrases using "drop." Then, write sentences using the phrases.

Phrases	Definitions
1. a drop in the bucket	*a small amount compared to the whole*
2. drop the ball	
3. at the drop of a hat	
4. Drop everything!	
5. drop out of (something)	

Did You Know? ◇◇◇◇◇◇◇◇◇◇

Stan Lee signed thousands of autographs, especially during the last part of his life. The price of a Stan Lee autograph was $50 in 2010 and $100 in 2016, and it can be worth over $150 today.

1. *The money he saves is **a drop in the bucket** considering his earnings from TV appearances.*

2. _____

3. _____

4. _____

5. _____

Read the following passage on the Marvel Multiverse. Then, do the exercises.

The MARVEL Multiverse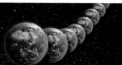

🎧 10

Stan Lee envisioned the Marvel Universe as a place where all his creations could coexist in one fictional realm. This is where Spider-Man, Iron Man, Captain America, the Fantastic Four, the Avengers, the Punisher, the Inhumans, the Silver Surfer, Daredevil, the Guardians of the Galaxy, and many other superheroes, supervillains, mutants, gods, and alien life forms fight it out for mastery of the Marvel Universe. Because the Marvel Universe is really a multiverse, its characters can exist in alternate universes and move back and forth between states of life and death, like in the case of Spider-Man and Captain America, who die on occasion only to come back to life.

Most of the action in the Marvel Universe takes place on Earth-616, where humans also exist. This number is also referred to as the Official Reality Number. Aside from the Marvel Universe, there is the Ultimate Marvel Universe, or Earth-1610. Things start to get a bit more complicated here as some characters that have died in the Marvel Universe are perfectly fine in the Ultimate Universe. At the same time, some characters that exist in the Marvel Universe do not exist in the Ultimate Universe. For instance, after the death of the Peter Parker Spider-Man in the Marvel Universe, the Marvel Ultimate Universe Spider-Man became a mixed-race Spider-Man named Miles Morales.

Finally, there is the Marvel Cinematic Universe, which contains all the Marvel characters owned by Marvel Studios and its parent company, Walt Disney, but excludes Spider-Man, which is owned by Sony, and the X-Men and the Fantastic Four, which are owned by Fox. Business, it seems, is also multiversal.

Making Inferences

Check (✓) the statements you think Stan Lee would agree with.

1. Stan Lee's idea of the Marvel Universe was a collection of fragmented fictional realms. ☐
2. Life and death are finite, irreversible states in the Marvel Multiverse. ☐
3. Events on Earth-616 are carbon copies of events occurring on Earth-1610. ☐
4. It is perfectly normal for Captain America to lend a hand to Iron Man if need be. ☐
5. Ironically, business can be as multiversal as the fictional world envisioned by Stan Lee. ☐

Reflections   Real-life superheroes are people who dress up in superhero outfits in order to perform community services such as community service or vigilantism—civilians engaged in fighting crime. Some real-life superheroes from around the world are the Chinese Redbud Woman, who dresses in a cape and mask and hands out food to Beijing's homeless, and the British Shadow, who dresses like a ninja and takes the fight to Yeovil's drug dealers and muggers. Does the world need more real-life superheroes, or should their work be best left to professionals?

Jerry Lawson:
Thinking
Out of the
Console Box

Unit Preview

A. Discuss the following questions.

1. Assuming that you have played a computer game at some point in your life, what is your favorite computer game? What makes this game interesting to you?

2. If you do play computer games, do you play them on your smartphone, computer, or game console? Which of these do you prefer and why?

B. Write definitions in English for the following words and expressions. Check your definitions again after reading the passage to make sure they fit the context of the passage.

1. in the know (*phr.*) _____

2. usher in (*phr.*) _____

3. heartland (*n.*) _____

4. hardwire (*v.*) _____

5. video arcade (*n.*) _____

6. quarter (*n.*) _____

7. cash in hand (*phr.*) _____

8. devise (*v.*) _____

9. rudimentary (*adj.*) _____

10. pronouncement (*n.*) _____

C. Test your knowledge on the topic of game consoles by checking Yes/No in the table below. After reading the passage, check whether your answers were correct or not.

Background Knowledge	True?	
	Yes	No
1. Nintendo was the first game console to use game cartridges.		
2. Microsoft invented the joystick when it designed the first XBox.		
3. Sony's Playstation was the first game console to use a microprocessor.		

11

Atari is credited as the first-generation video game console.

What did they mean?

1 Explain the following quote by Cave Johnson (from the game *Portal 2*): "Science isn't about why. It's about why not!"

Kudos to you[1] if you have heard of Gerald A. Lawson (1940-2011) or his most famous creation, the Fairchild Channel F video game console, though chances are that neither name will take many video game buffs on a trip down memory lane[2]. For the few in the know, Lawson was a technical whiz who helped usher in an industry worth hundreds of billions of dollars. Thanks in part to his vision and Channel F, millions of video gamers across the world today are playing *Minecraft*, *League of Legends*, *Super Smash Bros*, and loads of other such games on their X-Boxes, PlayStations, or Wii Us.

Lawson was born in Brooklyn and grew up in Queens, New York. While still a teenager, he built his own ham radio and occasionally earned pocket money by repairing TV sets. He later gave college a go but never earned a degree; instead, he moved to the San Francisco Bay area in 1970 and got a job as an engineer and designer at the Fairchild Camera and Instrument Corporation, a semiconductor maker. While it is true that Lawson's arrival in Silicon Valley was a natural consequence of his keen interest in electronics, his involvement in the field was rather groundbreaking, being one of a very few black engineers working in America's technological heartland at the time.

Before Lawson's arrival in Silicon Valley, first-generation computer game consoles such as Atari and the Magnavox Odyssey each had one game hardwired onto the printed circuit board of the console itself, allowing it to basically play only one game. Moreover, game consoles in those days were a luxury. The Magnavox Odyssey cost $100, which in 2020 money would be about $650. That was a lot of money to play just one game. A far more popular alternative for gamers of the day was the coin-operated video arcade game machine. One could keep dropping quarters in these video arcade machines and switching between games as long as the cash in hand lasted. The attraction was the wide choice of games these publicly installed machines offered.

Lawson, in fact, designed and built a coin-operated game machine in his garage—a game called *Demolition Derby*. But what Lawson and his team of engineers at Fairchild did for the game console industry is nothing short of revolutionary: they devised a way for a single game console to accommodate interchangeable game cartridges. Their Channel F creation came with a choice of game cartridges that could be swapped as easily as a cassette or CD. That essentially brought the whole video arcade inside the home of the computer game player.

A Fairchild Channel F Grandstand game console

Gamers could now gather around a home game console, play and swap games, and even trade them. The "F" in the Channel F stood for the fun that this game console brought to the home of each gamer who owned one.

Lawson was also instrumental in designing an easy-to-use and amazingly functional joystick for the Channel F game console at a time when these consoles had mostly rudimentary game controls: basically, keyboard buttons. More importantly perhaps, Lawson's team incorporated Fairchild's F8 microprocessor into the design of the Channel F against the pronouncement of many industry experts that microprocessors would not work in game consoles.

45

50

What did they mean?

2 Explain the following quote by Ezio Auditore (from the game *Assassin's Creed 2*): "Wanting something doesn't give you the right to have it."

A girl with virtual reality headset and joystick playing games

Many decades later, the names Fairchild and Channel F are largely unrecognizable, proof that great ideas do not guarantee economic success. Over time, Fairchild's games were unable to compete with the far more attractive ones developed by Atari, Nintendo, Sega, and others. As for Jerry Lawson, his name might not be well-known today, but it will not be forgotten tomorrow. Diehard gamers will make sure of that.

55

What did they mean?

3 Explain the following quote by Waka (from the game *Okami*): "Life is all about resolve. Outcome is secondary."

→ **IDIOMS:** Usage and Etymology ←

1 **kudos to you:** This idiom has the literal meaning of "You have earned my praise." The word "kudos" comes from Greek, and it means "glory" or "fame." The idiom was first used in English in 1812 in the sense of "fame resulting from an achievement."

2 **a trip down memory lane:** This idiom has the figurative meaning of "reminiscing over memories of past events," and it is mostly used to describe positive memories. The idiom can be found in the literature of the late-1800s and was popularized by a 1924 song titled "Memory Lane."

Reading Comprehension

Inference

1. Where in the passage would the following sentence fit best?

"By disproving the skeptics, Lawson again proved his technological insight."

a. at the end of the third paragraph

b. at the end of the fourth paragraph

c. at the end of the fifth paragraph

d. at the end of the last paragraph

Did You Know? ∞∞∞∞∞∞∞

After arriving in Silicon Valley, Jerry Lawson joined a home inventors club that included Steve Jobs and Steve Wozniak, the founders of Apple.

Detail

2. Which game console maker produced the least successful video games?

a. Nintendo   b. Fairchild   c. Sega   d. Atari

Detail

3. Which of the following statements about Jerry Lawson is true?

a. He moved to the San Francisco Bay area in 1970 after graduating from college.

b. He argued that microprocessors would not work in game consoles.

c. With his team, he designed a functional joystick for the Channel F game console.

d. He used to repair video game arcade machines in his youth in Queens, New York.

Vocabulary

4. Which word pair does NOT fit in with the others?

a. game console / cartridge   b. DVD player / compact disc (CD)

c. cassette player / cassette   d. personal computer / mouse

Vocabulary

5. Which of the following words is a synonym of the highlighted phrase in paragraph 2?

a. tried out   b. dropped out   c. gave up   d. renounced

Inference

6. Which of the following statements can be inferred from the passage?

a. Lawson's Demolition Derby coin-operated game machine was a huge success.

b. Lawson became very rich thanks to his technological innovations.

c. The Channel F was the most successful home game console of its time.

d. The video game arcade age was ended by swappable game cartridges.

Did You Know? ∞∞∞∞∞∞∞

As of 2020, black engineers comprised around one percent of the tech employees working in Silicon Valley.

Inference

7. Which of the following best relates to the theme of this passage?

a. "All programmers are playwrights, and computers are lousy actors." (Unknown)

b. "If your presence doesn't make a difference, your absence won't make a difference." (A.N. Rao)

c. "The real problem is not whether machines think but whether men do." (B.F. Skinner)

d. "My computer must be broken. Whenever I ask a wrong question, it gives the wrong answer." (A. Brilliant)

Proofreading and Writing Practice

A. Read the following passages. Find 5 mistakes in each paragraph and correct them.

1. Sidney K. Meier (born 1954) is ~~consider~~ *considered* by many to be the founding father of American computer games. Meier grew up in the U.S., where he enrolled from the University of Michigan with a degree in computer science. During a career to span nearly 30 years, he has developed some truly iconic computer games. To most gamers, the name Sid Meier is antonymous with *Civilization*, perhaps the best strategy game of all time. Sid Meier has been induced into the Academy of Interactive Arts and Sciences Hall of Fame.

2. Hideo Kojima (born 1963) is a Japanese game design legends. Kojima got his start in 1986 with Konami, where he designed the first edit of the game *Metal Gear*. Kojima's love for film helped him give the games he designed fascinated and complex plots. His storytelling ability is evident in *Metal Gear Solid*, a game that has achieved legend status among gamers. In 2019, Guinness World Records recognized Hideo Kojima for the video game director the most followed on Twitter and Instagram.

B. Video games are increasingly replacing literature in the lives of young gamers. Make an argument for the need to create more video games with content that draws from literature. Your argument should contain your opinion as well as supporting facts and should be around 150 words.

Vocabulary in Context

A. Complete the conversation below with vocabulary from the passage.

> quarters   cash in hand   ushered in   in the know

A: Seb, my retro video arcade machine has just arrived. Come on over!

B: Sure thing. I'll bring my piggy bank, too. It's full of coins.

A: Good because I've got no _____¹ at the moment. I've spent my last dollar on this machine.

B: You bought the first-generation *Pac-Man*, right?

A: I sure did. For those _____², it's the bestselling arcade game in history. Over 400,000 machines sold!

B: A true icon of the 1980s. It really _____³ the era of video games.

A: Are you impressed yet?

B: I'll let you know after I drop a few _____⁴ in it. I'm coming over now!

Did You Know? ◇◇◇◇◇◇◇◇◇◇

Jerry Lawson became increasingly opposed to violence in video games as he got older and made his feelings clear on this topic: "Most of the games that are out now—I'm appalled by them. To me, a game should be something like a skill you should develop. If you play this game, you walk away with something of value."

B. Choose the sentences where the underlined words have the same meanings as they do in the passage.

1.　a. Despite having only a rudimentary education, Tom became a multimillionaire.

　　b. The Aztecs built their pyramids by using only rudimentary tools.

2.　a. Some central processor units (CPUs) are hardwired onto circuit boards.

　　b. A fever is the body's hardwired response to an ongoing infection.

3.　a. The vice president made a name for himself in the American heartland.

　　b. Wall Street is the heartland of American commerce and trade.

C. Complete the chart below with definitions for the given phrases using "fall." Then, write sentences using the phrases.

Phrases	Definitions
1. fall on deaf ears	*to have no one listening to what is said or suggested*
2. fall for a line	
3. fall into step	
4. fall to pieces	
5. fall guy	

Did You Know? ◇◇◇◇◇◇◇◇◇◇

Jerry Lawson's accomplishments—the Channel F console and his technical papers—are exhibited at the World Video Game Hall of Fame in Rochester, New York.

1. *Jill's complaint about her broken window **fell on deaf ears**; the landlord left it as it was.*

2. _____

3. _____

4. _____

5. _____

Reading Connections

Read the following passage on the development of game consoles. Then, do the exercises.

🎧 12

A Timeline for the Development of Game Consoles

1972	The first official home game console is produced: the Magnavox Odyssey. The console lacked sound, so playing a game on it was like watching a silent movie. The graphics were also primitive.
1975-1977	Atari produces the PONG console, based on its popular PONG video arcade coin-operated machine. Magnavox launches two upgraded versions of its original Odyssey: the Odyssey 100 and 200. Atari launches the 2600 console. Coleco launches the Telstar console, which has color graphics and different difficulty levels for its games. Fairchild introduces the revolutionary Channel F, which flops due to its uninspired games.
1978-1980	The Atari 2600 continues its dominance. Nintendo enters the video game industry with the Color TV Game Series of consoles, which comes with features such as a steering wheel for driving or joysticks. Coleco also produces consoles for car racing, and pinball games, and even shooting—with a working gun controller—in an attempt to challenge the mighty Atari 2600.
1981-1990	This is referred to as the Golden Age of Video Gaming. Sega's SG-1000 (1983) console and Nintendo's NES (1983) dominate the decade with hit games such as *Pac-Man*, *Mario Bros*, *The Legend of Zelda*, and *Final Fantasy*. Coleco, Atari, and other console-makers are unable to keep up.
1991-1997	Game storage changes from cartridges to CDs. The increased capacity allows games to move from a 2D to a 3D format. New console makers Commodore, NEC, Panasonic, and even Apple, among others, come and go. Sony enters the market with its PlayStation (1994) while Nintendo offers a head-mounted display to view 3D graphics called Virtual Boy (1995).
1998-2004	Sega introduces the Dreamcast (1998) console, the first to provide a built-in modem for online playing. Microsoft enters the market with the well-received XBox (2001).
2005-2020	Nintendo brings Wii on the market in 2009. By this time, only three home console makers remain to battle it out for market share: Nintendo (Wii), Sony (PlayStation), and Microsoft (XBox). Their consoles and games now offer real-life graphics and real-time Internet operability as well as VR experiences.

Making Inferences

Check (✓) the statements you think a video game enthusiast would agree with.

1. Video game console-makers have maintained their market positions over the years. ☐

2. The Golden Age of Video Gaming was defined by the success of Nintendo and Sega's games. ☐

3. The functions of video game consoles have not changed much from the pre-2000 era. ☐

4. In the video game industry, great hardware equates to success in the market. ☐

5. Today, video gamers can use their consoles to play online against human opponents. ☐

<u>Reflections</u>   Is spending hours with a computer game any different from spending hours in front of a TV set? If so, which activity is more beneficial, and which one is more detrimental? Give a few reasons and, if possible, facts to back your claim.

Pininfarina Must Be Italian for Rembrandt

Unit Preview

A. Discuss the following questions.

1. What is your impression of the appearance of Italian supercars such as Ferrari and Lamborghini? Do you have a favorite Ferrari or Lamborghini model?

2. Does the design of a product such as a supercar have an impact on the value of the product? Do people spend more money in order to own a product defined by an exclusive design?

B. Write definitions in English for the following words and expressions. Check your definitions again after reading the passage to make sure they fit the context of the passage.

1. bread-and-butter (*adj.*) ....

2. fabled (*adj.*) ....

3. subsequently (*adv.*) ....

4. conglomerate (*n.*) ....

5. comprise (*v.*) ....

6. integrated (*adj.*) ....

7. exclusivity (*n.*) ....

8. restructuring (*n.*) ....

9. flair (*n.*) ....

10. one-off (*adj.*) ....

C. Test your knowledge on the topic of Pininfarina design by checking Yes/No in the table below. After reading the passage, check whether your answers were correct or not.

Background Knowledge	True?	
	Yes	No
1. Pininfarina is a luxury Italian car manufacturer.		
2. Pininfarina is famous for designing some of the most iconic Ferraris.		
3. The name Pininfarina comes from the name of the company's founder.		

1966 Alfa Romeo Spider

Carrozzeria Pininfarina S.p.A. is a comprehensive design agency engaged in product and industrial, architectural, general transportation, and especially automotive design—its bread-and-butter business since the company's foundation in 1930 by Battista "Pinin" Farina. When the company gets it right—and Pininfarina hardly gets it wrong—superlatives are not enough to describe a Pininfarina-designed product. What can be said, after all, about a 1966 Alfa Romeo Spider or the Ferrari 250 GTO? Perhaps only, "Hang them up on a wall in the Louvre and admire silently in awe."

For most of its fabled history, Pininfarina has been a family-controlled business. Pinin Farina kept the reigns[1] of his company until 1968, when he changed his last name to Pininfarina and then passed control to his son, Sergio. That year, the company also changed its name from Pinin Farina S.p.A. to Pininfarina S.p.A. The baton was subsequently passed[2] down to Battista's grandson, Andrea Pininfarina, in 2001, and to Andrea's younger brother, Paolo Pininfarina, in 2008. Family control of the business ended in 2015, when Indian conglomerate Mahindra & Mahindra acquired Pininfarina S.p.A. Paolo, however, retained his position as president of the design company after the takeover.

Almost a century after its founding, the company's design principles have remained loyal to Battista Farina's original vision: pure and elegant designs and innovative and long-lasting products. These days, the design studio's portfolio comprises a variety of projects that build on the successes of the Re 460 Swiss Railways locomotive and train (1991-97) design, the Casio G-Shock GE-2000 design, the Ferra Tower Singapore (2013) design, the Schaefer 800 (2013) superyacht design, the 2006 Olympic torch design, and many others. From Coca-Cola soda dispensers to integrated kitchen furniture and appliance designs, Pininfarina's stamp is a guarantee of quality, exclusivity, and stunning beauty.

That's quite a résumé for a company that started out as a coachbuilder, as its name *carrozzeria* (bodywork) signifies. Prior

What did they mean?

1 Explain the following Charles Bukowski quote: "If you're going to try, go all the way. It's the only good fight there is."

What did they mean?

2 Explain the following John Maeda quote: "Art is a question to a problem. Design is a solution to a problem."

The Olympic torch design by Pininfarina

to and following the Second World War, Pininfarina specialized in building coaches (bodies) for carmakers such as Alfa Romeo, Fiat, Nash-Healey, Cadillac, and Rolls-Royce. During the 1950s, Pininfarina entered a partnership with Ferrari and started producing the coaches for pretty much all of the superbrand's models. To keep up with increasing demand, Pininfarina had to add a second factory in 1955 and invest heavily in technology development. It actually became the first company in the world to build and use a wind tunnel (1972) for testing its automotive designs.

Pininfarina designed some of Ferrari's most iconic cars.

The 1980s and 1990s were both a blessing and a curse for Pininfarina. The company rapidly expanded its coach manufacturing capacity, adding a third factory in Italy and a fourth one in Sweden. Expansion, however, meant added debt, and when global markets crashed in 2008, Pininfarina found itself under a mountain of debt. The eventual restructuring meant the closure of its factories and the sale of the company to the conglomerate Mahindra & Mahindra. The blessing in all of this was a return to basics to what Pininfarina does best: offer design services characterized by unmatched flair and style.

The end of its automotive coach manufacturing activities has allowed Pininfarina to expand into fields such as architectural and industrial design as well as land and marine transport design. To be sure, Pininfarina still designs one-off cars and provides engineering solutions for global car manufacturers, which brings in about 80 percent of its current revenue. In 2020, the company even launched a new EV hypercar in celebration of its 90th anniversary. That is a young 90, and besides, the company's designs are already immortal. In the world of design, *Pininfarina* is Italian for Rembrandt.

What did they mean?

3 Explain the following M.C. Escher quote: "Only those who attempt the absurd will achieve the impossible."

→ **IDIOMS: Usage and Etymology** ←

1 **keep (hold) the reigns:** This idiom means figuratively "to be in control of a business or other organization," such as a political party. The idiom is based on the method of controlling a horse or a team of horses by pulling on the reins, which are long straps of leather attached to a horse's bit, in order to control the animal.

2 **pass the baton:** This idiom means figuratively "to hand over a particular duty or responsibility." The idiom alludes to a relay race in which one runner literally hands a baton to the next runner.

Reading Comprehension

Choose the best answers to the following questions on the passage "*Pininfarina* Must Be Italian for Rembrandt."

Inference

1. **Where in the passage would the following sentence fit best?**

   "And Rembrandt himself would probably agree with that assertion."

   a. at the end of the second paragraph

   b. at the end of the third paragraph

   c. at the end of the fifth paragraph

   d. at the end of the last paragraph

Did You Know? ∞∞∞∞∞∞∞∞

In the 1920s, Henry Ford invited Battista "Pinin" Farina to lunch and offered him the position of Ford's chief designer. Farina refused the offer and instead established his own company. The rest is automotive history.

Detail

2. **Which of the following products is outside Pininfarina's design portfolio?**

   a. architectural   b. marine transport

   c. multimedia   d. industrial

Detail

3. **Which of the following statements is NOT true according to the passage?**

   a. Pininfarina used to build coaches for Nash-Healey and Cadillac.

   b. Pininfarina designed a locomotive and a train.

   c. Pininfarina was bought by the conglomerate Mahindra & Mahindra.

   d. Pininfarina is presently producing EV hypercars at its four car factories.

Did You Know? ∞∞∞∞∞∞∞∞

Sergio Pininfarina (1926-2012), the son of Battista "Pinin" Farina, designed some of Pininfarina's most iconic cars, such as the 1984 Ferrari Testarossa. For his service, he was nominated in 2005 as "Senatore a vita"—an honorary senator for life in the Italian Senate.

Vocabulary

4. **Which word pair does NOT fit in with the others?**

   a. unmatched / flair   b. exclusive / style

   c. design / portfolio   d. stunning / beauty

Vocabulary

5. **Which of the following words is synonymous with the highlighted word in paragraph 1?**

   a. admonishments   b. praises   c. rebukes   d. reprimands

Inference

6. **What lessons can be learned from Pininfarina's 1980s expansion?**

   a. Investment in production growth always pays off in the long run.

   b. Companies need to continue to expand in order to remain profitable.

   c. It was a bad idea to expand the company after the 2008 market crash.

   d. Expansion financed through debt can lead to financial ruin.

Inference

7. **Which of the following quotes best describes Pininfarina's design philosophy?**

   a. "The alternative to good design is always bad design." (Adam Judge)

   b. "Everything should be made as simple as possible, but not simpler." (Albert Einstein)

   c. "Art is anything you can get away with." (Marshal McLuhan)

   d. "Look at usual things with unusual eyes." (Vico Magistretti)

Proofreading and Writing Practice

A. Read the following passages. Find 5 mistakes in each paragraph and correct them.

1. Pininfarina's Heritage Tower is located ~~on~~ *in* the Itaim Bibi area of Sao Paulo, Brazil. The residential tower

highlights the design studio successful partnership with the renowned Cyrela development brand. The project

brings together elegant and innovation in the design of an imposing landmark in downtown Sao Paulo. The

Heritage's design was expired by the shape of a Pininfarina-designed supercar. Living in this building means

quite literally living in the lop of luxury.

2. Pininfarina used a car design concert in the design of the X95 "Superfly" yacht. The luxury yacht is build and

marketed by the renowned British vessel builders Princess Yachts. The innovative design combines a sleak,

dynamic exterior with ample outdoor space and an open-plan, modular interior. The idea behind Pininfarina's

design are to give boat owners a flexible boating experience. The name Superfly recalls to the yacht's skybridge

deck, which offers a 360-degree view and generous deck spaces.

B. Make an argument for sacrificing practicality in favor of appearance in high-end design. Your argument should contain your opinion as well as supporting facts and should be around 150 words.

Vocabulary in Context

A. Complete the conversation below with vocabulary from the passage.

> fabled   comprises   bread-and-butter   conglomerate   restructuring

A: Have you heard? The auto plant is shutting down. Everyone will be laid off.

B: It's in the news. The parent company is undergoing _____¹. It took some heavy losses due to the downturn in the economy.

A: The parent company is a global _____², right?

B: Yes, it is. It _____³ some 40 smaller companies.

A: Still, auto manufacturing was its _____⁴ business, wasn't it?

B: Well, it still is. It's just closing a few factories in some countries.

A: It's just bad luck for our city to lose such a big employer.

B: Not just a big employer but also a _____⁵ car manufacturer.

A: True. Its name and reputation need no introduction.

B. Choose the sentences where the underlined words have the same meanings as they do in the passage.

1. a. Calls for racially integrated schools in segregated areas of the U.S. emerged in the 1950s.

    b. Microchip designers are now developing integrated memory and processing solutions.

2. a. This club maintains its exclusivity by adhering to a members-only policy.

    b. The boutique hotel down the street places an emphasis on exclusivity and luxury.

3. a. One could say that Jimmy has always had a flair for learning languages.

    b. Part of the job requirement for a model is to always dress with flair.

C. Complete the chart below with definitions for the given phrases using "off." Then, write sentences using the phrases.

Phrases	Definitions
1. off the record	*speaking unofficially or unrecorded*
2. off the cuff	
3. off the deep end	
4. off-color remark	
5. off one's rocker	

1. *The government official gave the information about the upcoming vote **off the record**.*

2. _____

3. _____

4. _____

5. _____

Read the following passage on the fastest street car on the planet. Then, do the exercises.

The Fastest Street Car on the Planet

Chalk up another triumph for Pininfarina. It has just built the fastest street-legal car on the planet, and it is an EV (electric vehicle). Pininfarina unveiled its 1,900-horsepower EV monster at the 2019 Geneva Motor Show and aptly named it the Battista in homage to the company's founder, Battista "Pinin" Farina. The Battista's stats are mind boggling: a top speed of 480kph, an acceleration of 0-100kph in two seconds, a range of 450km on a full charge, and, oh, a price tag of a cool 2.5 million U.S. dollars. On performance alone, the Battista gives back a lot in return for the money. First of all, this is truly a hypercar—a rarefied category of cars that puts even the Ferraris and the Lamborghinis of the world to shame. And if that is not enough, this particular $2.5-million hypercar is a Pininfarina, which basically makes it a work of art. The lines of the car's design flow sensuously in classic Italian style, without sharp or intrusive edges or shapes. The design is as clean and suave as you would expect from Pininfarina, yet it is also subtly innovative: the car's tail spoiler is uniquely split and doubles as an air brake, which is sorely needed to bring this automotive hurricane to a stop. The doors are butterfly style while the interior is plush with fine Italian leather. Yet for all its thunder, the Battista is an environmentally friendly mode of transportation, having a pollution factor of zero. The model is slated to enter a limited production of 150 units in 2020, the year of Pininfarina's 90th anniversary. Mahindra and Mahindra, the parent company, plans to continue making EV hypercars under the brand Automobili Pininfarina, so expect it to keep fighting to retain its "fastest street-legal car on the planet" badge in the future.

Making Inferences

Check (✓) the statements you think a supercar enthusiast would agree with.

1. Pinin would be proud to see that the car named after him retains his design principles. ☐
2. Despite its smooth curves, there is nothing particularly innovative about the Battista's design. ☐
3. The Battista would surely outpace any model of Ferrari or Lamborghini supercars. ☐
4. Environmentalists would feel uncomfortable getting behind the wheel of a Battista. ☐
5. The Battista is a one-of-a-kind work of art valued at 2.5 million U.S. dollars. ☐

Reflections   As of 2019, auto manufacturers around the world had pledged to spend some 225 billion dollars for the development of electric vehicles. EVs are increasingly displacing traditional fossil-fuel-powered cars in terms of price, performance, and naturally, eco-friendliness. By the year 2030, will the world of automobiles have gone completely electric or will gasoline- and diesel-powered cars still be trudging along the roads and highways of this near future?

4

Industrial Design B

The Eternal House of BVLGARI

Unit Preview

A. Discuss the following questions.

1. What are your favorite jewelry or accessory luxury brands? Do you own a luxury brand item? If so, what is it?

2. Can you name some Italian luxury brands? Have you heard of the BVLGARI brand? What does BVLGARI make?

B. Write definitions in English for the following words and expressions. Check your definitions again after reading the passage to make sure they fit the context of the passage.

1. chic (*adj.*)

2. affluent (*adj.*)

3. silversmith (*n.*)

4. bric-a-brac (*n.*)

5. unbridled (*adj.*)

6. pinnacle (*n.*)

7. stylized (*adj.*)

8. cabochon (*n.*)

9. horology (*n.*)

10. behemoth (*n.*)

C. Test your knowledge on the topic of the BVLGARI brand by checking Yes/No in the table below. After reading the passage, check whether your answers were correct or not.

Background Knowledge	True?	
	Yes	No
1. BVLGARI was established by a Bulgarian man in the late 1800s.		
2. The first BVLGARI store was opened on 5th Avenue in Manhattan.		
3. BVLGARI is a partner in a chain of high-end hotels and resorts.		

BVLGARI is famous for its jewelry, watches, perfumes, and leather goods.

What did they mean?

1 Explain the following old proverb: "Gold cannot be pure, as people cannot be perfect."

What did they mean?

2 Explain the following quote by Salvador Dalí: "The difference between false memories and true ones is the same as for jewels: it is always the false ones that look the most real, the most brilliant."

Mention the name Bulgari, and images of glamorous divas adorned in golden jewelry set with sensuously colorful stones flood to mind: Elizabeth Taylor, Sofia Loren, Audrey Hepburn, and pretty much any notable Hollywood star or high-fashion supermodel. BVLGARI— spelled with a "v" to pay homage to[1] its Roman roots—is an iconic luxury brand that has stood for more than a century for fine Italian jewelry craftsmanship and has provided majestically chic designs to its affluent clients the world over.

The House of BVLGARI was founded in 1884 by Sotirio Boulgaris (1857-1932), the son of a family of Greek silversmiths who emigrated to Italy. There, Boulgaris changed his surname to Bulgari and established his first shop selling precious metals, antiques, jewels, and bric-a-brac at via Sistina 85—the first location of the brand BVLGARI. Throughout the decades, the House of BVLGARI has continued to expand its fame internationally through unbridled creativity and innovative use of materials in its designs while drawing inspiration from the monuments and decorative motifs of Rome, the Eternal City.

Sotirio Bulgari ran his business in the family. His sons Giorgio and Costantino joined him in growing his jewelry design house from a few shops that sold Roman-themed silver ornaments to English vacationers in Rome to an international luxury brand that produced the pinnacles of sophistication in high-end jewelry.

In the 1920s, BVLGARI made use of platinum and diamonds for its jewelry and set them in geometric and stylized Art Déco designs. After the Second World War, it introduced yellow gold, spiraling it in coils for its Serpenti (snake) designs. During the Dolce Vita era of the 1950s and 60s, BVLGARI started combining chromatic precious stones with colored ones in its designs as well as the cabochon motif, inspired by the cupolas of the Eternal City. The Monete (coin) was also introduced in the 1960s, and it featured jewelry made from antique coins surrounded by diamonds and gemstones. These reproduction coins were engraved with the names of Roman emperors.

BVLGARI's classic "Serpenti" designs

By the 1970s, the design house had established a presence all over Europe as well as the U.S., as the third generation of the Bulgari family owners started launching more daring designs that included Far East motifs and even Pop Art. Around this time, the design house made its move into the horology business with a stunning classic: the BVLGARI BVLGARI watch. The inspiration for the timepiece came from Roman coins. The engraving of the name brand around the watch face recalled the engravings on ancient coins.

BVLGARI diversified its portfolio in 1993 with the founding of Bulgari Parfums in Switzerland, which oversaw the production of all its fragrances, including its initial offering, Eau Parfumée Au Thé Vert. Riding high on its success, BVLGARI went public in 1995, when it was listed on the Milan Stock Exchange. The design house saw 150-percent growth between 1997 and 2003, and in 2011, it signed a strategic alliance with LVMH SA, the world's leading luxury group. That transaction, worth 5.2 billion dollars, ended the family ownership structure of BVLGARI, giving LVMH a controlling 51-percent stake in the design house.

For BVLGARI, there is no time like the present[2]. The design house employs over 4,000 people around the world, making it a behemoth as well as an icon of the luxury design industry. Paolo Bulgari (born 1937), a great-grandson of Sotirio Bulgari, is currently the president of BVLGARI, ensuring that the family name remains strongly associated with a legacy that started and has continued to grow in the Eternal City for over 135 years.

What did they mean?

3 Explain the following quote by Kahlil Gibran: "Perhaps time's definition of coal is the diamond."

→ **IDIOMS: Usage and Etymology** ←

1 **pay homage to:** This idiom has the figurative meaning of "to copy or emulate someone or something in content or style as a way of honoring or showing respect toward it." The idiom is based on the 13th-century French word *homage*, which was a "ceremony or act of acknowledging one's faithfulness to a feudal lord."

2 **no time like the present:** This idiom has the literal meaning of "the best time to do something is right now." The idiom comes from a proverb first written in 1562. The idea behind the proverb is that if you wait too long, you may never get to do the thing you want to accomplish.

Reading Comprehension

Choose the best answers to the following questions on the passage "The Eternal House of BVLGARI."

Inference • **1. Where in the passage would the following sentence fit best?**

"The story of BVLGARI does not stop in its eminent past."

a. at the beginning of the first paragraph

b. at the beginning of the second paragraph

c. at the beginning of the fourth paragraph

d. at the beginning of the last paragraph

Detail • **2. Which of the following is NOT a BVLGARI design motif?**

a. Cabochon   b. Monete

c. Sistina   d. Serpenti

Detail • **3. Which of the following statements is true about BVLGARI BVLGARI?**

a. It was the third generation of BVLGARI's stunning watch designs.

b. It heralded the end of BVLGARI's involvement in the horology business.

c. Its design was inspired by ancient Roman coins.

d. Its design includes Far East and Pop Art motifs.

Vocabulary • **4. Which word pair does NOT fit in with the others?**

a. notable / stars   b. glamorous / divas

c. high-fashion / supermodels   d. affluent / clients

Vocabulary • **5. Which of the following words is an antonym of the highlighted phrase in paragraph 4?**

a. original   b. copy   c. duplicate   d. remake

Inference • **6. Which of the following statements can be inferred from the passage?**

a. BVLGARI's reputation among Hollywood stars had no effect on its brand value.

b. Rome's symbols have been essential to the appeal of BVLGARI's creations.

c. BVLGARI's listing on the Milan Stock Exchange reduced the brand's attraction.

d. After its takeover, LVMH ended the Bulgari family's affiliation with BVLGARI.

Inference • **7. Which of the following best relates to the theme of this passage?**

a. "Jewelry takes people's minds off your wrinkles." (Sarah Phillips)

b. "Get rid of everything that is not essential to making a point." (Christoph Niemann)

c. "One does not put oneself in place of the past; one only adds a new link." (Paul Cézanne)

d. "Men shop to get what they want; women shop to find out what they want." (Unknown)

Did You Know? ◇◇◇◇◇◇◇◇◇◇

In 1975, BVLGARI sent a limited-edition watch with the inscription "BVLGARI ROMA" to its top 100 clients as a Christmas gift. The success of this campaign assured the company that it should proceed with the launch of its legendary BVLGARI BVLGARI watch.

Did You Know? ◇◇◇◇◇◇◇◇◇◇

BVLGARI's creations have appeared in over 40 films, including *Casino*, starring Sharon Stone, and *Mission Impossible*, starring Tom Cruise.

Proofreading and Writing Practice

A. Read the following passages. Find 5 mistakes in each paragraph and correct them.

1. Sotirio Boulgaris was born in ~~Greek~~ _{*Greece*} in 1857 to a large family of 11 children. In 1880, he immigrated to Italy in search for a better life, with only a few cents to his name. His ability to work valuable metals and stones into expired jewelry enabled Sotirio to work as a silversmith in Rome. Sotirio's passionate for his craft led to the establishment of BVLGARI stores across Italy. As well as growing the brand, Sotirio had a huge hand in establishing its aesthetical.

2. The first BVLGARI Hotel is schedule to open in Tokyo in early 2023. The hotel will join a string of BVLGARI-branded luxury travel destinations stretching from Milan until Bali. BVLGARI Tokyo will occupy the top seven floors of a skyscraper due to raise in the Yaesu 2-Chome North District. The hotel will be located within walk distance of the imperial palace. The hotel's design has faithfully recreated BVLGARI's aesthetic of high Italy craftsmanship and artistic sophistication.

B. High-end jewelry and watch makers are blurring the lines between art and functionality with products that can be afforded by a small number of people. Make an argument for returning functional art to the masses. Your argument should contain your opinion as well as supporting facts and should be around 150 words.

Vocabulary in Context

A. Complete the conversation below with vocabulary from the passage.

> chic   cabochon   stylized   silversmiths   bric-a-brac

A: Meg, I'm in the mood for shopping, and I just got paid!

B: Sounds like a plan. I'm in the market for some new rocks. I'm thinking about a diamond ring for my B-day. Something _____[1] and full of style.

A: I know this fancy little shop that sells all kinds of vintage _____[2].

B: Let's check it out then. What are you in the mood for?

A: I was thinking of some sort of a ring with a large stone in the shape of a _____[3]. Maybe a ruby or an emerald.

B: My mom has a ton of those. She said they were popular in the 50s and 60s.

A: I know. _____[4] used to polish them by hand back then. It was a true art form. I'm not sure if they still do that nowadays.

B: Some probably still do. But all new designs are much more _____[5]. Realism has truly disappeared.

B. Choose the sentences where the underlined words have the same meanings as they do in the passage.

1. a. Jenny has just moved to an affluent neighborhood thanks to her mom's new job.

    b. The source of this tiny affluent of the Colorado River is hard to pinpoint.

2. a. Horology enthusiasts will happily snatch up a vintage Philippe Patek timepiece.

    b. The science of horology has seen great advances during the atomic age.

3. a. The Behemoth described in the book of Job was probably inspired by a hippopotamus.

    b. Mining dump trucks are behemoths on wheels that can haul as much as 460 tons.

C. Complete the chart below with definitions for the given phrases using "kick." Then, write sentences using the phrases.

Phrases	Definitions
1. kick the habit	*to give up an addiction or harmful practice*
2. a kick in the face	
3. kick around an idea	
4. kick the bucket	
5. kick up one's heels	

1. *He had smoked for 50 years before finally **kicking the habit** after suffering a heart attack.*

2. _____

3. _____

4. _____

5. _____

Read the following passage on superstars that wear BVLGARI jewelry. Then, do the exercises.

Jeweler to the
HOLLYWOOD SUPERSTARS

🎧 16

The beauties of Rome's present and past have been translated by BVLGARI into timeless jewelry creations that have for many decades decorated the fingers, wrists, and necks of the beauties of Hollywood. The relationship started during the Dolce Vita era of the 1950s and 60s, when Hollywood began producing extravagant films in Rome, such as *Roman Holiday*, *La Dolce Vita*, and *Cleopatra*. The glamorous and charismatic women who starred in these movies—Audrey Hepburn, Grace Kelly, Elisabeth Taylor, Ingrid Bergman—took an instant liking to the BVLGARI store on *via dei* Condotti (Condotti Street), and in fact established a lifelong love affair with the luxury jewelry brand, showing their passion for its products on and off the screen. Elisabeth Taylor (1932-2011), who owned one of the most extensive jewelry collections in the world, even claimed in her book *My Life in Jewelry* that "one of the biggest advantages to filming *Cleopatra* in Rome was BVLGARI's shop."

The list of Hollywood and international superstars who have worn BVLGARI on screen and at events such as the Oscars or the Cannes and Venice film festivals over the years is extensive to say the least. BVLGARI's arresting designs have appeared in no fewer than 40 films. Who can forget the image of Sharon Stone surrounded by BVLGARI-designed jewelry in the movie *Casino*, the appearances of actress Charlize Theron wearing an iconic Serpenti necklace and matching bracelet and earrings at the 91st Academy Awards, or actress Naomi Watts wearing a BVLGARI necklace with cabochons at the 2016 Cannes Film Festival?

BVLGARI, for its part, has been buying back at public and private auctions many of its iconic jewelry pieces that had belonged to screen sirens such as Elisabeth Taylor and Gina Lollobrigida and has continued to decorate a new generation of superstars with these eternally dazzling pieces. Jessica Chastain, for example, was seen wearing Elizabeth Taylor's formal octagonal sapphire necklace at the Cannes Film Festival in 2013. BVLGARI even held a 2019 exhibition at the Castel Sant'Angelo and at the National Museum of the Venice Palace featuring jewelry pieces previously owned by Elisabeth Taylor as well as the role of the design house during Rome's Dolce Vita era.

Julianne Moore
wearing a BVLGARI
necklace

Making Inferences
Check (✓) the statements you think an employee of BVLGARI would agree with.

1. BVLGARI jewelers have drawn inspiration for their designs from Hollywood movies. ☐

2. The Dolce Vita period jumpstarted the love affair between Hollywood stars and BVLGARI. ☐

3. Images of Hollywood divas wearing BVLGARI have increased the mystique of the brand. ☐

4. Hollywood star Jessica Chastain bought and wore some jewelry of icon Elisabeth Taylor. ☐

5. BVLGARI is highly interested in preserving and showcasing its history and past creations. ☐

Reflections   The prices of high-end jewelry are out of reach for ordinary people, yet this is precisely why they dream of owning such exclusive creations. It can even be said that the higher the cost, the higher the desirability of owning a high-end piece of jewelry. If this is true, what are people really attracted to: the beauty of luxury products, their exclusivity, or perhaps their material value?

The Glam Rebels Against the Rock Rebellion

Unit Preview

A. Discuss the following questions.

1. Do you listen to rock 'n roll? If so, is there a particular rock 'n roll genre that you enjoy listening to? What are some of your favorite rock 'n roll bands?

2. Who is an influential rock 'n roll musician that you know and admire? What attributes do you admire about this particular musician?

B. **Write definitions in English for the following words and expressions. Check your definitions again after reading the passage to make sure they fit the context of the passage.**

1. drab (*adj.*)

2. counterculture (*n.*)

3. espouse (*v.*)

4. throng (*n.*)

5. defection (*n.*)

6. androgynous (*adj.*)

7. caricature (*n.*)

8. over-the-top (*adj.*)

9. mercurial (*adj.*)

10. despot (*n.*)

C. **Test your knowledge on the topic of glam rock by checking Yes/No in the table below. After reading the passage, check whether your answers were correct or not.**

Background Knowledge	True?	
	Yes	No
1. Glam rock was a musical movement that started in the United States.		
2. Glam rockers popularized the androgynous look that typified their appearance.		
3. One of the UK's most famous glam rock musicians was Freddie Mercury of Queen.		

In 1971, British musician Marc Bolan and his band T. Rex were invited on the British TV music show *Top of the Pops* to perform their new number, "Hot Love." Those were the days when young people commonly listened to rock 'n roll bands such as the Who, Pink Floyd, and Led Zeppelin, who composed complex tunes with resonating power chords and virtuoso guitar and drum solos and performed them in static stage acts characterized by dull styling and drab costuming. In their four minutes and 17 seconds on *Top of the Pops*, Marc Bolan and T. Rex unleashed glam rock upon a stunned audience, standing the existing rock 'n roll counterculture on its head[1].

Bolan emerged on the *Top of the Pops* stage in yellow satin pants and a black shirt with green and red fringe and with wild hair curls and teardrops of glitter placed under his eyes, creating a coy, half-ironic image that perfectly complemented the song's catchy pop melody and "la-la-la" refrain. Glam rock became, at that very moment, a celebration of glamour, fame, and excess that flew in the face of England's existing economic troubles. Bolan and T. Rex had just pulled on the masks of youthful illusion, slyly poking fun at the seriousness and authenticity espoused by the mature grown-beard bands of the rock 'n roll rebellion.

The following morning, as throngs of teen girls and boys all across England applied glitter to their faces, the glam rock revolution was set in motion. And as "Hot Love" climbed to the top of the British music charts, musicians from all genres started their defection to glam rock, essentially taking the glam rebellion in three directions. The initial one was the silly, glittery, sexy, and fun type of music shown on TV by T. Rex. Musicians such as Sweet adopted and elevated this aesthetic of androgynous looks and catchy melodies with repetitive hooks to a subgenre that came to be known as glitter.

Glam rock's more artistic and perhaps theatrical side was soon formulated by David Bowie and Roxy Music. Whereas glitter was all about the surface and less concerned with the music itself, musicians such as Bowie were more ambitious in their musical and lyrical pursuits, often exploring a darker side of their psyche that lay buried beneath the glitzy layers of makeup and transvestite wardrobes. Bowie went as far as to replace himself with a

The visual styles of glam rock are often characterized as androgynous.

What did they mean?

1 Explain the following Truman Capote quote: "Certain shades of limelight can wreck a girl's complexion."

What did they mean?

2 Explain the following John Berger quote: "The happiness of being envied is glamour."

conjured-up glam rock persona named Ziggy Stardust—a theatrical, sexually ambiguous, narcissistic caricature of a rocker. Bowie's 1972 album *The Rise and Fall of Ziggy Stardust and the Spiders from Mars* spent two years on the British musical charts.

A third, more mainstream direction was taken by British band Queen and American band Kiss and musician Alice Cooper. These musicians applied the glam rock aesthetic—outrageous costumes, stage performances, and androgynous looks—to their own brands of heavy rock music, resulting in over-the-top celebrations of the rock star itself. In this sense, Queen lead singer Freddie Mercury will forever be remembered as the ultimate champion of rock concerts. Draped in ridiculous-looking outfits—imagine tight white leather pants, naked torso, and a king's crown—Freddie somehow managed to look mercurial as he dominated and commanded his audiences with the authority of a despot.

By the mid-1970s, glam rock started to vanish, giving way to punk, heavy metal, and other youthful rebellions. David Bowie had already retired his alter ego Ziggy Stardust at the conclusion of a 1973 live concert, pushing glam rock into a musical no-man's land[2] and thus foretelling its impending end, appropriately, with a wink.

Glam rock had a big influence on the American rock band Kiss.

45

50

55

What did they mean?

3 Explain the following David Bowie quote: "Fame can take interesting men and thrust mediocrity upon them."

→ **IDIOMS: Usage and Etymology** ←

1 **stand something on its head:** The figurative meaning of this idiom is "to make people think about something in a completely different or new way." The figurative meaning is derived from the literal meaning of the expression "to stand something upside-down." The implication is that by turning something upside-down, you can see it—and think about it—from a different perspective.

2 **no man's land:** This idiom, popularized in World War I, means "the area between the front lines of entrenched armies" or "an area outside anyone's control." The idiom comes from the 14th century Old English word "Nonemanneslond," used for the site of executions outside the north wall of London.

Reading Comprehension

Choose the best answers to the following questions on the passage "The Glam Rebels Against the Rock Rebellion."

Inference
1. Where in the passage would the following sentence fit best?

"As its name implies, this type of music was not thematically complex."

a. at the end of the second paragraph

b. at the end of the third paragraph

c. at the end of the fourth paragraph

d. at the end of the fifth paragraph

Detail
2. Which of the following is NOT a characteristic of glam rock?

a. grown beards   b. transvestite wardrobes

c. repetitive hooks   d. alter egos

Detail
3. Which of the following statements is NOT true according to the passage?

a. David Bowie's music explored the darker side of the human psyche.

b. Freddie Mercury looked ridiculous in his over-the-top stage outfits.

c. Sweet's melodies were catchy and light themed.

d. Marc Bolan launched glam rock on *Top of the Pops*.

Vocabulary
4. Which of the following words does NOT fit in with the others?

a. coy   b. narcissistic   c. dominating   d. despotic

Vocabulary
5. Which of the following is synonymous with the highlighted word in paragraph 5?

a. garnished   b. groomed   c. embellished   d. decked out

Inference
6. What can be inferred about glam rock from the passage?

a. Its disappearance owes to the lack of musical talent of its performers.

b. It was a youthful rebellious fad that melted away as quickly as it came.

c. Its end signified the end of all youthful music rebellions.

d. The elements of its aesthetic never transcended glam rock.

Inference
7. Which of the following quotes would best apply to a glam rocker?

a. "Lies don't end relationships; the truth does." (Shannon L. Alder)

b. "Nice people don't necessarily fall in love with nice people."
   (Jonathan Franzen)

c. "I don't care what you think unless it is about me." (Kurt Cobain)

d. "Confidence is the prize given to the mediocre." (Robert Hughes)

Did You Know? ◇◇◇◇◇◇◇◇◇◇

T. Rex's "Hot Love," the song that launched the glam rock movement, took Marc Bolan and his band only 10 minutes and four of bottles of brandy to write. The music itself is basically a 12-bar blues melody.

Did You Know? ◇◇◇◇◇◇◇◇◇◇

British musician Elton John appeared on the *Top of the Pops* show in 1973 wearing sparkly orange sunglasses as he performed "Goodbye Yellow Brick Road." This prompted some commentators to label him a glam rocker. The label, rightfully, did not stick on Elton John for too long.

Proofreading and Writing Practice

A. Read the following passages. Find 5 mistakes in each paragraph and correct them.

1. Some early glam rockers combined elements of bubblegum pop with elements of psychedelic rock to create

a brand of music that had a sexually ~~charging~~ *charged* feeling. The effect was amplified by over-the-top costumes that

displaced with the accepted norms of gender in fashion. Makeup, eyeliner, glitter, satin, skin-tight pants, and

the whole spectrum of colors has become part of every male performer's wardrobe. Long, feminine-looking hair

was also optional, and it was complemented by feminine gesturing and high-pitched vocals. Glam rock artists

were essentialy cross-dressers.

2. In 1977, Marc Bolan returned to music after a hietus of a few years during which he fathered a son with singer

Gloria Jones. The glam rocker recorded a new album titled *Dandy in the Underworld* with a completely revamp T.

Rex band. Bolan and the new-looks T. Rex began a short tour of the UK in 1977, inviting the band the Damned

on their tour. Together, the two bands performed a hard-hitting, punk-like rondition of T. Rex's song "Get It On."

Their performance signified the passing of the musical baton from glam to punk with Bolan orchestrating the

hand over.

B. Make an argument for the influence of glam rock on the music industry in your own country. Your argument should contain your opinion as well as supporting facts and should be around 150 words.

Vocabulary in Context

A. Complete the conversation below with vocabulary from the passage.

| drab | counterculture | over-the-top | androgynous | throngs |

A: This year's spring collection looks so _____¹; there are no colors whatsoever.

B: What did you expect? PD's never been known for _____² designs.

A: No, I didn't expect anything exaggerated from her, of course. But come on. Give the _____³ of followers something to cheer for...

B: I'm actually disappointed, too. I expected a stronger statement.

A: Right? Where's PD's revolutionary spirit?

B: I'm afraid those days are long gone. The _____⁴ has now become the establishment, and her latest designs prove that beyond doubt.

A: Still, she did maintain the _____⁵ look in all the designs.

B: Call me cynical, but was it out of practicality more than anything else?

A: Sure, you can double the money if you can sell them to both women and men.

Did You Know?

When asked about the title of his song "Vicious"—a song that had influenced many glam rockers—Lou Reed recalled that it had been inspired by Andy Warhol, who suggested for the song's theme a type of viciousness similar to when one "is hit by a flower."

B. Choose the sentences where the underlined words have the same meanings as they do in the passage.

1.   a. Edwin had <u>espoused</u> Mary at the request of his, and especially her, parents.

b. The concept of a spherical Earth had been <u>espoused</u> by the Greeks as early as 6 B.C.

2.   a. It is now believed that this odd-looking meteor is of <u>mercurial</u> origin.

b. Napoleon was known for his <u>mercurial</u> presence on the battlefield.

3.   a. Of history's heinous <u>despots</u>, none was more savage than Pol Pot.

b. Jose Mourinho is often described as a coach with a <u>despot</u> mentality.

C. Complete the chart below with definitions for the given phrases using "over." Then, write sentences using the phrases.

Phrases	Definitions
1. fork something over	*to give something you don't want to give*
2. get over oneself	
3. over the hump	
4. over the hill	
5. over the moon	

Did You Know?

The synthpop movement of the early 1980s, which included bands such as Duran Duran and Human League, was inspired by glam rock, which also inspired a myriad of long-haired, aqua-net and spandex pop-metal bands such as Def Leppard, Poison, and Bon Jovi during the late-1980s.

1. *"Now **fork over** your wallet," the thief demanded with a threatening look on his face.*

2. _____

3. _____

4. _____

5. _____

Read the following passage on five glam rock hit songs. Then, do the exercises.

Five Unforgettable Glam Rock Hits

🎧 18

Other than the obvious T. Rex hit "Hot Love," which launched the glam rock revolution, the following five glam hits have stood the test of time with audiences, musicians, and critics alike. The classification is strictly chronological, as each one of these hits is a classic in its own right.

Roxy Music, "Virginia Plain" (1972): Lead singer Bryan Ferry's vocals formed an out-of-this-world partnership with Eno's synthesizer work, creating a musical manifesto for the glam rock generation: "So me and you / Just we two / Got to search for something new."

Lou Reed, "Vicious" (1972): Lou Reed's opening song on his second album starts out with lyrics inspired by Andy Warhol: "Vicious—You hit me with a flower / You do it every hour / Oh, baby you're so vicious." The album was produced by David Bowie.

David Bowie, "The Jean Genie" (1972): David Bowie took the musical genie out of the 1960s R&B bottle with this one. Mick Ronson supplied the buzzing guitar work. The lyrics, meanwhile, are rife with gay double entendres—a trademark of the genre and of early Bowie in particular.

Mott the Hoople, "All the Young Dudes" (1972): David Bowie collaborated with some material, helping Mott write a song that references the Beatles and the Rolling Stones in its hard-hitting, generation-defining message: "Oh, is there concrete all around / Or is it in my head?"

The Sweet, "The Ballroom Blitz" (1973): The Sweet were the archetypal glam rock band, and this may very well have been their archetypal song. The hard, rhythmical guitar riffs and quaintly unconventional vocals are a perfect fit for the over-the-top costumes. Long live glam rock!

Making Inferences
Check (✓) the statements you think a music critic would agree with.

1. "Virginia Plain" and "The Ballroom Blitz" were characterized by subdued and wonted vocals. ☐
2. Andy Warhol's production of Lou Reed's second album assured the success of "Vicious." ☐
3. David Bowie drew inspiration for "The Jean Genie" from an R&B song from the 1960s. ☐
4. Lou Reed and Mott the Hoople owe some of their musical success to David Bowie. ☐
5. Glam rock groups and musicians were disconnected from each other in their creative efforts. ☐

Reflections Today's pop music industry is becoming increasingly fixated on appearance, much like in the days of glam rock. Is this another passing fad, or has the quality of the music become forever irrelevant?

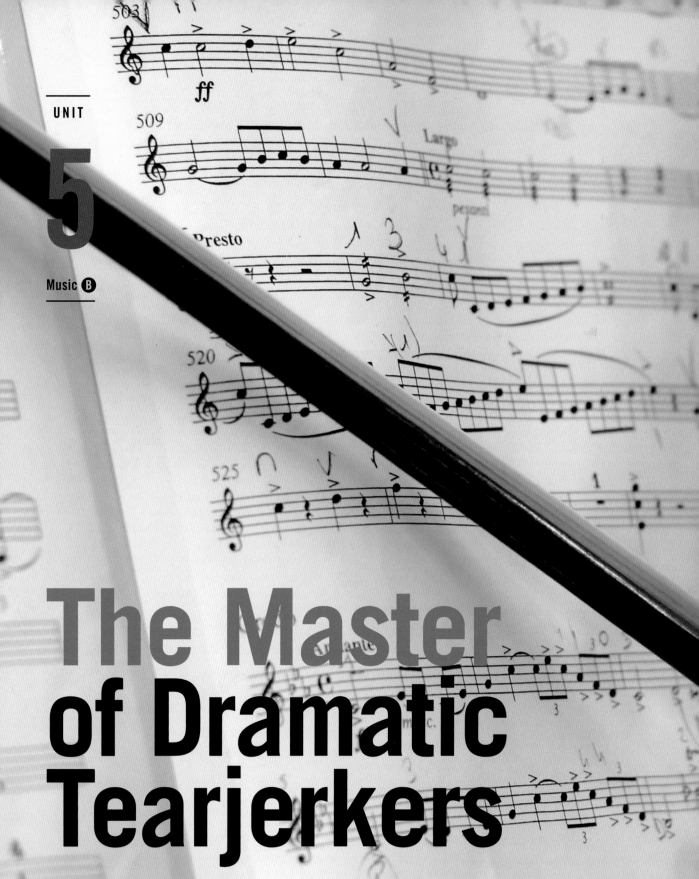

The Master of Dramatic Tearjerkers

Unit Preview

A. Discuss the following questions.

   1. Have you ever seen an opera performed live or on some form of media? If so, what is your favorite opera?

   2. Do you know the names of some renowned opera composers? If so, who is your favorite opera composer? Do you know the period of time during which your favorite composer lived?

B. Write definitions in English for the following words and expressions. Check your definitions again after reading the passage to make sure they fit the context of the passage.

   1. score (*n.*)

   2. manipulator (*n.*)

   3. tearjerker (*n.*)

   4. libretto (*n.*)

   5. titan (*n.*)

   6. with bated breath (*phr.*)

   7. evoke (*v.*)

   8. adverse (*adj.*)

   9. deferential (*adj.*)

   10. can't hold a candle to (*phr.*)

C. Test your knowledge on the topic of Giacomo Puccini and his operas by checking Yes/No in the table below. After reading the passage, check whether your answers were correct or not.

Background Knowledge	True?	
	Yes	No
1. Giacomo Puccini and Wolfgang Amadeus Mozart were good friends.		
2. Puccini's *Madame Butterfly* was inspired by a novel.		
3. All of Puccini's operas enjoyed great success when they premiered.		

19

Statue of Italian opera composer Giacomo Puccini

Audiences have been secretively or openly wiping away tears during a night at the opera ever since an Italian named Jacopo Peri penned a musical composition titled *Dafne* in 1590. From this early era through the following four centuries, Western-style operas have become ever more structurally, stylistically, and musically elaborate. Composers such as George Frideric Handel (1685-1759), Wolfgang Amadeus Mozart (1756-1791), or Giuseppe Verdi (1813-1901) have inked their names to some of the most accomplished opera scores of the Baroque, Classical, and Romantic periods. Among these eminent musicians, the last great Romantic composer, Giacomo Puccini (1858-1924), stands out as the greatest manipulator of the human heart. He was the undisputed master of the dramatic tearjerkers.

Puccini composed scores such as *La Bohème* (1896), *Tosca* (1900), and *Madame Butterfly* (1904) at a time when Romanticism, an artistic and literary movement that championed emotions over the scientific conformity of the Enlightenment and the ensuing Industrial Revolution, prevailed across Europe. Compared to the Baroque-style operas that preceded them, Romantic operas involved expanded orchestras of up to 100 players and monumental supporting choruses, and they added dramatic elements in everything from costumes to scenic artistry. Puccini also incorporated realist—*verismo* in Italian—subject matter in his creations, such as the marital problems, illnesses, and fallings in and out of love by the odds and sods[1] of the Italian society.

Puccini and the other verismo composers of his time drew their inspiration for the human dramas explored in their operas from plays and novels. *Madame Butterfly*, for instance, was inspired by the French novel *Madame Chrysanthème*, written by Pierre Loti. Aside from the thematic inspiration, Puccini also benefitted from the help of two brilliant individuals: Luigi Illica and Giuseppe Giacosa, the librettists who wrote the librettos to his greatest operas.

When discussing Puccini's musical style, perhaps a comparison to Richard Wagner—another titan of the Romantic period—might be useful. While Wagner produced operas of epic length—the *Ring* takes about 15 hours to perform—his music has been said to be "better than it sounds." That backhanded compliment[2] could very well be code for tediousness, depending

What did they mean?

1 Explain the following quote by Victor Hugo: "In the opera we call love, the libretto is almost nothing."

What did they mean?

2 Explain the following quote by George Bernard Shaw: "Opera is when a tenor and soprano want to make love but are prevented from doing so by a baritone."

Scene from *La Bohème*, composed by Puccini

Scene from Puccini's final opera, *Turandot*

upon who you ask. Puccini, on the other hand, infused a constant musical high tension in his works that worked up his audiences and kept them with bated breath. Add to that his natural Italian flair for the dramatic and a poet's imagination that allowed him to evoke dreamlike moods, and you start to understand why *La Bohème* is everyone's secret favorite opera.

La Bohème premiered in 1896 in Turin and was based on *Scènes de la Vie de Bohème*, a collection of connected stories by Henri Murger. Though not an immediate success, its blend of sentimental scenes and accessible conversational style soon made it a favorite among popular audiences. *Tosca*, Puccini's first experimentation with verismo, premiered in 1900 in Rome and received a highly enthusiastic response from the Roman audience. *Madame Butterfly*, meanwhile, premiered in 1904 in Milan to adverse critical reviews, prompting Puccini to make heavy revisions to the premiere version. The improved rendition debuted in Brescia a few months later, where it was received with great acclaim.

La Fanciulla del West (The Girl of the Golden West), which Puccini described as a "second *Bohème* but stronger, bolder, vaster," premiered at the Met in New York in 1910 to polite reviews, but despite its deferential treatment, it was obvious that *La Fanciulla* couldn't hold a candle to *La Bohème*. And though Puccini would continue to write operas until his death in 1924, the well of tears, it seemed, had already run dry for the great master of dramatic tearjerkers.

What did they mean?

3 Explain the following quote by Robert Benchley: "Opera is when a guy gets stabbed in the back, and instead of dying, he sings."

→ **IDIOMS: Usage and Etymology** ←

1 **odds and sods:** This British idiom has the figurative meaning of "miscellaneous bits and pieces" and is derived from the old Anglo-Saxon "odds-and-ends," meaning scraps. When applied to people, the expression means "a miscellaneous or assorted group of people."

2 **backhanded compliment:** This idiom has the figurative meaning of "a condescending compliment" or "an insult disguised as praise." The idiom is derived from the 17th-century synonymous expression "left-handed compliment." The word "left"—*sinister* in Latin—means "evil" or "wrong." On the other hand, the term "backhand," in use since the late 1800s, means "devious" or "sarcastic."

Reading Comprehension

Inference

1. Where in the passage would the following sentence fit best?

"A night at the opera, as everyone knows, means a night of shedding tears."

a. at the beginning of the first paragraph

b. at the beginning of the third paragraph

c. at the end of the fifth paragraph

d. at the end of the sixth paragraph

Did You Know? ∞∞∞∞∞∞∞∞

Women were prohibited from singing on stage during the 17th century. Their roles would be sung instead by castrated males—*castrati* in Italian. The era's most famous castrati was Baldassare Ferri, and he was so adored that audiences would fill his carriage with flowers after a performance.

Detail

2. Which of the following is NOT the name of an opera?

a. *Madame Chrysanthème*
b. *Dafne*
c. *La Fanciulla del West*
d. *Tosca*

Detail

3. Which of the following statements is NOT true about Giacomo Puccini?

a. He wrote his operas during the Romantic period of the musical genre.

b. He wrote the librettos to his operas based on realist subject matter.

c. He had a poetic mind and an innate inclination toward the dramatic.

d. His operas have a more popular appeal than Wagner's compositions.

Did You Know? ∞∞∞∞∞∞∞∞

The voice of an opera singer has a different sound frequency from musical instruments. For this reason, opera singers can project their voices over the sound of a full orchestra.

Vocabulary

4. Which word pair does NOT fit in with the others?

a. realist / subject matter
b. dreamlike / moods
c. scenic / artistry
d. thematic / inspiration

Vocabulary

5. Which of the following is an antonym of the highlighted phrase in paragraph 4?

a. agitated
b. roused
c. pacified
d. excited

Inference

6. Which of the following statements can be inferred from the passage?

a. Puccini incorporated the elements of verismo in his very first opera.

b. Audiences do not enjoy sentimentalism during a night spent at the opera.

c. Music critics were not fully candid in their reviews of *La Fanciulla del West*.

d. Puccini's greatest masterpieces were written after 1910.

Inference

7. Which of the following best relates to the theme of this passage?

a. "Literature spends its evenings at the opera." (Radu H. Hotinceanu)

b. "Actors are the only honest hypocrites." (William Hazlitt)

c. "That's how we stay young these days: murder and suicide." (Eugene Ionesco)

d. "Logic will take you from A to B. Imagination will take you everywhere." (Albert Einstein)

Proofreading and Writing Practice

A. Read the following passages. Find 5 mistakes in each paragraph and correct them.

1. The word opera is a̶ *the* Latin plural form of *opus*, which means "work." The orchestral induction to an opera is known as an overture. An opera *buffa* (comic), such as Gaetano Donizetti's *Don Pasquale*, is usually a comic type of opera timed on the lives of ordinary people. An opera *seria* (serious), such as George Frideric Handel's *Demofoonte*, implores themes from religion, mythology, or history with characters such as gods or ancient heroes. An operetta is a musical comedy with the characters speaking their lines but also singing a number of songs toward the performance.

2. Giacomo Puccini was destined to become a composer. His father, Michele, was an organist and choirmaster as good as a composer of operas and symphonic pieces. His mother, Albina, was also a musicalist. Albina's musician brother, Fortunato, lives with the family and became Puccini's first teacher. In this rather bohemia family, there would be no escape from music for young Puccini. Though he covered music from his family, Puccini discovered his passion for becoming a composer at the Instituto Musicale, where he studied Giuseppe Verdi's *Rigoletto*, *La Traviata*, and *Il Trovatore*.

B. Make an argument for the need for governments to provide support for the arts. Your argument should contain your opinion as well as supporting facts and should be around 150 words.

Vocabulary in Context

> deferential   can't hold a candle to   titan   manipulator   tearjerker

A: What are your first impressions on the movie?

B: It was a bit of a ....¹; half the audience was teary eyed at the end.

A: I guess it's expected from this director. He's a known ....² of audiences, given his tendency toward overly sentimental plots.

B: Well, it fits my movie taste, for sure. I'm a hopeless romantic.

A: So how does it rate compared to your other romantic comedy favorites?

B: That's a different story. Unfortunately, it ....³ my all-time favorite, *Four Weddings and a Funeral*.

A: And the lead actress? She's considered a ....⁴ of the industry. Was she worth the price of admission?

B: Considering the quality of the supporting cast, she delivered a competent performance.

A: That's a rather ....⁵ statement. Now tell me what you really thought.

Did You Know? ∞∞∞∞∞∞∞

The world's most famous opera house—La Scala in Milan (opened in 1778)—has the world's toughest audiences, who would not hesitate to make a performer sing until he got it right. Placido Domingo, however, received applause for half an hour and a standing ovation at La Scala—an extreme rarity—on December 15, 2019.

B. Choose the sentences where the underlined words have the same meanings as they do in the passage.

1. a. This <u>score</u> may be your best composition ever; the music is simply compelling!

    b. The <u>score</u> at halftime gave the home team every reason to believe they can win.

2. a. Scientists at the South Pole have to conduct experiments in extremely <u>adverse</u> weather conditions.

    b. The jury was presented evidence <u>adverse</u> to the claims made by the defendant.

3. a. Your poem needs to more skillfully <u>evoke</u> the sensory details of the location described.

    b. The ghost hunter prepared to <u>evoke</u> whatever spirits may have haunted the house.

C. Complete the chart below with definitions for the given phrases using "head." Then, write sentences using the phrases.

Phrases	Definitions
1. head trip	*thinking too much of oneself*
2. head-emptier	
3. head-spinning	
4. head-in-the-sand	
5. heads will roll	

Did You Know? ∞∞∞∞∞∞∞

The audience burst into laughter when 330-pound Luigi Lablache (1794-1854), cast in *La Traviata* as a prisoner held in a jail cell, sang the words, "I'm starving."

1. *Josie's been on a big **head trip** ever since she got on the American Idols show.*

2. ....

3. ....

4. ....

5. ....

Read the following passage on the life of Giacomo Puccini. Then, do the exercises.

Puccini's Life of Opera

 20

When Oscar Wilde wrote that "life imitates art far more than art imitates life," he certainly did not reference the life of Giacomo Puccini, but had he done so, he would not have been far off the mark.

Puccini lived a life of scandal, jumping from one affair to the next, even as he maintained a relationship with Elvira Gemignani—a married woman who would become pregnant with Puccini's son while still married to her husband. Elvira gave birth to Puccini's son, Antonio, in 1886, but was only free to marry Puccini after her husband was killed in 1904.

Puccini's marriage to Elvira did not stop him from continuing to have affairs with a number of women, particularly singers in his operas. One of his notorious affairs was a five-year entanglement with Blanke Lendvai, with whom she fell in love in Budapest in 1906 while attending a performance of his *Madame Butterfly*.

While most of Puccini's love affairs were real, at least one was imagined. Elvira accused one of Puccini's maids of having a liaison with her master. It was an accusation that despaired the maid so deeply that she took her own life. Elvira's claim was later proved untrue, and though she was found guilty of slander, she was spared from being sent to prison.

Puccini did take a break from his life of affairs, though not entirely of his own accord. In 1903, as Puccini, Elvira, and Antonio were being driven home on an icy road, their car skidded, crashed, and overturned in a field by the side of the road. Elvira and Antonio escaped injury, but Puccini suffered a broken thigh, which confined him to bed for a painful period of six months. As soon as this brief interlude from love ended, however, Puccini was already on the lookout for the next bed to jump into.

True to a life of opera, Elvira was aware of Puccini's never-ending romances but stayed with him to the very end, which came as a result of a heart attack on October 29, 1924. The ending was itself a bit of a tearjerker, as Puccini whispered his last words to Elvira. On that cold October morning at 11:30 a.m., Puccini's life of opera came, befittingly, to a remarkably artistic end.

Making Inferences

Check (✓) the statements you think a Giacomo Puccini biographer would agree with.

1. Puccini's life was not unlike the life of a Hollywood star: dramatic and full of excesses. ☐

2. Oscar Wilde's quote is a moral justification for living a life of excesses. ☐

3. Of all the women in his life, Elvira was the one who mattered the most to Puccini. ☐

4. Elvira was probably indifferent to Puccini's romantic escapades. ☐

5. One can see a bit irony in Puccini's death, being that he was killed by his own heart. ☐

Reflections   Many of the world's most acclaimed artists, writers, and musicians lived lives that were less than morally upright, to say the least. In a way, creativity requires a life less ordinary as ordinary lives cannot provide an artist with inspiration for the unusual. But if people require and expect artists to produce the unusual, should they be more tolerant and less judgmental when it comes to artists' personal lives and their lifestyles? Or should artists be held to the same moral standards as the rest of society?

A Cybernetic Bill of Rights

Unit Preview

A. Discuss the following questions.

1. What is the most surprising job in which robots are already at work replacing and even outperforming humans?

2. Can you think of an instance of a recent event where an AI-driven machine surpassed the ability of a human being?

B. Write definitions in English for the following words and expressions. Check your definitions again after reading the passage to make sure they fit the context of the passage.

1. crossroads (*n.*) ....
2. govern (*v.*) ....
3. grasp (*n.*) ....
4. frame of reference (*phr.*) ....
5. acuity (*n.*) ....
6. den (*n.*) ....
7. dehumanize (*v.*) ....
8. riddle (*v.*) ....
9. concur (*v.*) ....
10. higher entity (*n.*) ....

C. Test your knowledge on the topic of cybernetics by checking Yes/No in the table below. After reading the passage, check whether your answers were correct or not.

Background Knowledge	True?	
	Yes	No
1. Cybernetics deals with the construction and operation of robots in automation.		
2. Humans and animals are protected by certain rights.		
3. AI machines have achieved the ability to feel and display emotions.		

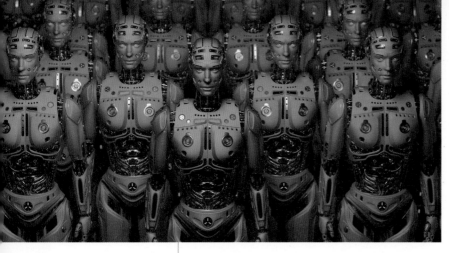

21

Humans have reached a crossroads in their technological advancement, having firmly stepped into the Cybernetic Age without even coming to an agreed terminology for the concept of cybernetics. Should the term cybernetics be applied to concepts describing artificial entities with artificial souls, or should cybernetics describe entities that preserve a human soul, or consciousness, within an artificially created organism?

The former case would involve robots governed by artificial intelligence (AI) whereas the latter would involve robots governed by a human brain (a robot's brain in which the memories and consciousness—the soul—of a human being have been transferred). A discussion on cybernetics, however, would be futile without a clear grasp of what it means to be human in the first place.

People have an intuitive understanding of what it means to be human, whether that understanding comes from a religious frame of reference or a scientific one. This understanding is not a universal one. Generally speaking, even within groups that are unified by a system of thought, few people can fully see eye to eye on what characteristics or combinations of traits are required to make a being human. Does intelligence suffice? Or should intelligence be complemented by the ability to feel emotion? Moreover, should a being have a straight moral compass[1] in order to be considered human? And not least of all, is belief in God a defining prerequisite?

Intelligence on its own is not solely a human trait. Animals display varying degrees of reasoning, as do AI machines. Feats of animal acuity have even astounded the scientists studying these animals. From dolphins that call each other by unique names to groups of elephants completing coordinated tasks and from chimps defeating adult humans at memory-based games to octopi displaying a keen sense for aesthetics in decorating their dens, intelligence is plentiful in the animal kingdom. Animals are also capable of

What did they mean?

1 Explain the following George Orwell quote: "If liberty means anything at all, it means the right to tell people what they do not want to hear."

Should AI entities have the same rights as humans?

feeling and displaying emotion as well as empathy.

As for morality, AI machines can learn and strictly abide by moral conventions, and many animal populations have been shown to abide by moral codes. Meanwhile, certain groups of people defined by status, ethnicity, or ideology regularly dehumanize other groups and cast them as lower or even undesirable. Even in advanced societies, groups of socially disadvantaged people such as the homeless are often viewed as sub-humans by some members of the more privileged classes. In fact, human history has been riddled by examples of group dehumanization that have led to slavery, ethnic cleansing, and even genocide.

One day, robotic machines will need to have their own set of rights.

If being human is hard enough to define, things do not get any easier when robots are thrown in the mix. The main problem for humans and machines alike is how to perceive and define consciousness or even life itself: When does life begin for a human, and when does it end? Science and religion do not concur on the subject. As for machines, who is to decide how long they may be allowed to "live"? And what exactly is consciousness? Such questions venture into the murky waters of philosophy.

Humans have already established certain animal rights, though they are clearly insufficient to protect countless species from inevitable extinction. As for robotic machines, they are still finding their feet[2]. Assuming that one day they will achieve some form of consciousness or self-awareness and the ability to feel and display emotions—and perhaps even the capability of believing in a higher entity—then they will need to have their own set of rights. Call it the Cybernetic Bill of Rights. That day is soon coming, and humans ought to start thinking about what those rights might be.

What did they mean?

2 Explain the following quote: "The next evolutionary step for humankind is to move from human to kind."

What did they mean?

3 Explain the following Grace Hopper quote: "The most damaging phrase in the language is, 'It's always been done that way.'"

→ **IDIOMS: Usage and Etymology** ←

1 **have a straight moral compass:** The compound noun "moral compass" refers figuratively to "an internalized set of values and objectives that guide a person with regard to ethical behavior and decision-making." Having a straight moral compass therefore means to have a morally upright set of such values. The first usage of this idiom was recorded around 1840.

2 **find one's feet:** This idiom means figuratively "to become comfortable with a new situation or experience." In a literal sense, it means to be able to stand up and walk, as newborns must find their feet. The idiom has been around since ancient times.

Reading Comprehension

Choose the best answers to the following questions on the passage "A Cybernetic Bill of Rights."

Inference

1. Where in the passage would the following sentence fit best?

"But understanding what defines us is not exactly a stroll in the park."

a. at the end of the second paragraph

b. at the end of the third paragraph

c. at the end of the fifth paragraph

d. at the end of the sixth paragraph

Did You Know? ∞∞∞∞∞∞∞∞∞∞∞∞∞∞

Cyborgs are humans with machine parts. Jesse Sullivan became the world's first "Bionic Man" cyborg in 2001, when his damaged arms were replaced by robotic prosthetics connected to his nervous system and controlled by his mind. His artificial limbs allow him to sense the temperatures of the objects he touches and handles.

Detail

2. Which of the following definitions can be applied to the term cybernetics?

a. human entities with artificial souls

b. human entities with human souls

c. artificial entities with human souls

d. artificial entities without souls

Detail

3. Which of the following statements is NOT true according to the passage?

a. Intelligence is a characteristic that does not belong solely to humans.

b. Animals have been shown to be capable of abiding by strict moral codes.

c. Science and religion disagree on the time when human life begins and ends.

d. Robotic machines have achieved a form of self-awareness.

Vocabulary

4. Which word or group of words does NOT fit in with the others?

a. consciousness   b. ethnic cleansing   c. genocide   d. dehumanization

Vocabulary

5. Which of the following is synonymous with the highlighted word in paragraph 6?

a. clear   b. cloudy   c. rapid   d. shallow

Inference

6. What can be inferred about the purpose of a Cybernetic Bill of Rights?

a. It guarantees that all living entities enjoy the same rights as humans.

b. It guarantees certain basic rights to all living entities.

c. It guarantees that animals, humans, and robots are equal.

d. It guarantees that extinction can no longer occur.

Did You Know? ∞∞∞∞∞∞∞∞∞

Some 300 people around the word have an implant in their chests that vibrates when they face north. The implant, called North Sense, is essentially a compass that helps these body-hackers find their bearings when they get lost.

Inference

7. Which of the following quotes best describes the idea of human rights?

a. "Man is not free unless government is limited." (Ronald Reagan)

b. "The history of liberty is the history of resistance." (Woodrow Wilson)

c. "Democracy is two wolves and a lamb voting on what to eat for lunch." (Marvin Simkin)

d. "The rights of every man are diminished when the rights of one man are threatened." (J.F.K.)

Proofreading and Writing Practice

A. Read the following passages. Find 5 mistakes in each paragraph and correct them.

1. Scientists have been ~~advanced~~ *advancing* the field of cybernetics by performing surgical implants of microchips onto the human brain surface. These implants allow humans to control their robotic limbs—artificially arms or legs—by using their thoughts. The key to controlling artificial limbs by using the mind has to know with neural decoding—translating the signals sent by the human neurons into machine language. This conversion is returned to as a neural-to-technological interface. Advanced interfaces of the future will need to connect to all the neurons in the human's brain.

2. The terms liberty and democracy are sometimes confused and used interchangeable. However, these two terminology do not convey the same meaning. Democracy refers to the people's right to participate in open and fair elections in order to elevate public officials. These elected officials would then make political decisions on their behalves based on majority rule. Liberty, meanwhile, refers to certain rights that cannot be removed by any majority vote or rule. These rights were discussed by James Madison as "unalienable" in the Declaration of Independence.

B. Make an argument for ensuring that individual liberties are not lost to the will of the majority under a democratic process. Your argument should contain your opinion as well as supporting facts and should be around 150 words.

Vocabulary in Context

A. Complete the conversation below with vocabulary from the passage.

| acuity | grasp | frame of reference | dehumanize | higher entity |

A: Hey, Keana. What are you reading?

B: It's a book on the reasons why people _____¹ their fellow human beings.

A: Personally, I can't _____² how people can do such horrible things to others.

B: And to themselves, apparently.

A: You really need a different _____³ to understand the psychology behind it.

B: It sounds like a challenging read.

A: It is. But I can really appreciate the author's _____⁴ on the subject.

B: So is there any hope for humanity, short of divine intervention from a _____⁵?

A: Yes, the author proposes some strategies for overcoming dehumanization.

B. Choose the sentences where the underlined words have the same meanings as they do in the passage.

1. a. Deep changes in weather patterns indicate that we are at an environmental crossroads.

   b. You'll see a tall glass building just after you drive past the next two crossroads.

2. a. The bank robbers' car was riddled by bullets as it attempted a getaway.

   b. The company is unfortunately riddled with counterproductive practices and attitudes.

3. a. After retiring from his trading job, Matt opened a hidden drinking and gambling den.

   b. The hiker decided to spend the night in what looked like a bear's den.

C. Complete the chart below with definitions for the given phrases using "hot." Then, write sentences using the phrases.

Phrases	Definitions
1. hot potato	*an issue that no one wants to deal with*
2. hot under the collar	
3. hot to trot	
4. all hot and bothered	
5. in hot water	

1. *The issue of raising taxes is a bit of a **hot potato**, so neither candidate addressed it fully.*

2. _____

3. _____

4. _____

5. _____

Read the following passage on the U.S. Bill of Rights. Then, do the exercises.

🎧 22

The U.S. Bill of Rights:
Liberty and Equality for All?

Bill of Rights

The original Constitution of the United States did not include many of the rights and liberties that Americans hold dear today, such as the freedoms of speech and religion and the right to a fair trial. These rights had to be included in the first 10 Amendments to the Constitution, known collectively as the Bill of Rights, which was written by James Madison and ratified by Congress in 1791.

While the Bill of Rights did not exclude any citizens from its protections, it was actually not intended to include large groups of people. Native Americans were considered aliens in their own lands and were therefore not protected by the U.S. Constitution. Neither were slaves. The U.S. Constitution, during the first 78 years after it was ratified, protected the right to own slaves and considered racial subordination legal. Slaves were therefore not governed by the U.S. Constitution but rather by a set of slave codes. Women were another group excluded from the protection of the Bill of Rights as they were considered second-class citizens who could not vote or own property. Similar to slaves, women were in fact the property of their husbands.

In time, these groups of people won their Constitutional rights guaranteed under the Bill of Rights, but not without a Civil War and long periods of struggle. The 13th Amendment to the Constitution, ratified in 1865, abolished slavery while the 15th Amendment, ratified in 1870, gave African Americans the right to vote. Women would have to wait until 1920 to win their right to vote, which came with the ratification of the 19th Amendment. Meanwhile, Native Americans finally earned the right to become citizens in 1924. Native Americans and African Americans, however, could not vote freely in every state of the U.S. until 1965 due to various barriers and regulations that disqualified them from exercising this fundamental right.

Making Inferences
Check (✓) the statements you think a civil rights historian would agree with.

1. The U.S. Constitution was flawed in its original ability to guarantee liberty and equality for all. ☐

2. Native Americans were considered Americans by the original U.S. Constitution. ☐

3. African Americans were governed by special slave codes described in the Bill of Rights. ☐

4. The U.S. Constitution gave women the right to vote before giving it to African Americans. ☐

5. African Americans had to wait close to 100 years to be allowed to freely vote in all states. ☐

Reflections　People have a very poor record of being fair to one another as history has demonstrated time and time again. If the past is an indication of things to come, what are the chances that a Cybernetic Bill of Rights will call for equality between humans and machines? And would such equality even be desirable?

The River-People Fight Back

Unit Preview

A. Discuss the following questions.

   1. What are the most important rivers in your country? Are there any special laws protecting them?

   2. What are the biggest challenges to a clean environment in your country?

B. Write definitions in English for the following words and expressions. Check your definitions again after reading the passage to make sure they fit the context of the passage.

   1. regime (*n.*)

   2. articulate (*v.*)

   3. commodity (*n.*)

   4. enshrine (*v.*)

   5. amendment (*n.*)

   6. guardian (*n.*)

   7. be intertwined with (*phr.*)

   8. onus (*n.*)

   9. mayhem (*n.*)

 10. embryonic (*adj.*)

C. Test your knowledge on the topic of legal rights for rivers by checking Yes/No in the table below. After reading the passage, check whether your answers were correct or not.

Background Knowledge	True?	
	Yes	No
1. In some countries, rivers enjoy the same rights as human beings.		
2. In New Zealand, it is illegal to drink water from rivers.		
3. In Bangladesh, a river is considered to be a mother to all citizens.		

The Whanganui River in New Zealand

In his 1974 book *Should Trees Have Standing? Toward Legal Rights for Natural Objects*, University of Southern California law professor Christopher D. Stone argued that natural features such as rivers could not be owned and had the right to appear in court if given a "legal personality." Stone's idea flew in the face of[1] Western tradition, which had regarded nature according to a property-based ownership regime until his publication. The idea itself, though novel from a legal perspective, articulated what indigenous people across the world had believed for thousands of years: that nature deserves human respect and protection as opposed to being regarded as a commodity to be owned, transformed, degraded, or even destroyed.

The idea of granting waterways "environmental personhood" is presently a growing movement across the world. In 2008, Ecuador became the first country to enshrine the legal rights of nature in its Constitution, and in 2011, Bolivia passed a similar amendment to its Constitution. In 2017, New Zealand became the first country to grant a specific river legal rights, while in 2019 Bangladesh became the first country to grant all of its rivers the same legal status as the country's citizens.

When the New Zealand government awarded the Te Awa Tupua River legal personhood in 2017, it officially recognized the river as an ancestor of the Whanganui Maori, an indigenous tribe of people native to New Zealand's Northern Island. The law appointed two guardians to defend the rights of the river: the New Zealand government and the Whanganui Maori. From a legal perspective, any act that harmed the river would be interpreted as causing harm to the tribe itself. To the Whanganui Maori, who believe that the *tupuna* (ancestors) continue to live in natural features such as mountains, forests, or rivers, this legislation was a triumph which gave hope to other people around the world whose lives are closely intertwined with rivers.

The Bangladeshi consider rivers to be their mothers.

Bangladesh is a country whose entire territory comprises delta land. The Bengal Delta is made up of the waterways of several river systems, including the Ganges and Brahmaputra rivers. The Bangladeshi naturally consider rivers to be their mothers in a quite literal sense. A 2019 Bangladeshi Supreme Court ruling recognized this physical and spiritual interdependence, guaranteeing that anyone accused of harming a river could be sued in court by the government-appointed National River Conservation Commission and tried as if that person had harmed his own mother.

Having laws in place that protect the rights of the world's River-People has made a virtue of necessity[2]. The difficulty here is their enforcement, as the onus of upholding the laws falls on the guardian, the entity representing the interests of the River-Person, be it the government itself, an NGO, a government-appointed body, or even a group of people. But these entities may not always have the desire or financial resources to engage in lawsuits. Also problematic is the fact that these guardians would be responsible for the actions of the River-People. What happens, for example, when a River-Person floods an area and kills human beings and destroys property? Is the guardian to be held responsible for the death and mayhem caused?

The movement of granting environmental personhood to the world's rivers is still in its embryonic phase. There is much to be learned and debated, but a universal Bill of Rights for the world's River-People would only make the life of every human more enjoyable, uplifting, and healthier. When that day comes, all of us would be able to take a page out of Whanganui Maori culture and say, "I am the river; the river is me."

What did they mean?

2 Explain the following quote by Mahatma Gandhi: "Earth provides enough to satisfy every man's needs but not every man's greed."

What did they mean?

3 Explain the following quote by Chris Maser: "What we are doing to the world's forests is but a mirror reflection of what we are doing to ourselves and to one another."

→ **IDIOMS: Usage and Etymology** ←

1 **fly in the face of:** This idiom has the figurative meaning of "going against accepted belief." The expression alludes to the literal act of a hen flying in the face of a dog, fox, or other animal that attacks it.

2 **make a virtue of necessity:** This idiom has the figurative meaning of "making the best of a difficult situation." The expression was first used by William Shakespeare in his play *Two Gentlemen of Verona*, in Act 4, scene 1.

Reading Comprehension

Choose the best answers to the following questions on the passage "The River-People Fight Back."

Inference • **1. Where in the passage would the following sentence fit best?**

"The severity of the punishment is a strong deterrent against river pollution."

a. at the end of the first paragraph

b. at the end of the second paragraph

c. at the end of the fourth paragraph

d. at the end of the fifth paragraph

Did You Know? ∞∞∞∞∞∞∞

The Te Awa Tupua River is not the only natural feature to have legal personhood in New Zealand. Mount Taranaki—a volcano sacred to the Maori—and Te Urewera Park—home to the Tuhoe people—have also been granted legal personhood status.

Detail • **2. Which of the following entities has NOT been granted legal personhood?**

a. the Te Awa Tupua

b. the Ganges

c. the Maori tupuna

d. the Brahmaputra

Detail • **3. Which of the following statements is true about the Whanganui Maori?**

a. They are the legal guardians of New Zealand.

b. They are the legal guardians of the Bengal Delta.

c. They are the legal guardians of the tupuna.

d. They are the legal guardians of the Te Awa Tupua River.

Vocabulary • **4. Which word pair does NOT fit in with the others?**

a. property / degraded

b. asset / transformed

c. estate / destroyed

d. mayhem / killed

Vocabulary • **5. Which of the following is synonymous with the highlighted phrase in paragraph 6?**

a. behave well

b. misbehave

c. behave similarly

d. behave in an opposite manner

Inference • **6. Which of the following statements can be inferred from the passage?**

a. Legally protected rivers will be protected from causing harm to humans.

b. Giving rivers legal status can improve the quality of human life.

c. Legal personhood for rivers amounts to an increase of human rights.

d. A Bill of Rights for the world's River-People would cause human mayhem.

Did You Know? ∞∞∞∞∞∞∞

Russia has more rivers than any other country in the world—over 100,000 of them. Bangladesh, known as "the land of rivers," has 700.

Inference • **7. Which of the following best relates to the theme of this passage?**

a. "The environment is everything that isn't me." (Albert Einstein)

b. "The poetry of the earth is never dead." (John Keats)

c. "How sad to think that nature speaks and mankind doesn't listen." (Victor Hugo)

d. "We must begin thinking like a river if we are to leave a legacy of beauty and life for future generations." (David Brower)

Proofreading and Writing Practice

A. Read the following passages. Find 5 mistakes in each paragraph and correct them.

1. The idea of giving nature ~~benefits~~ *rights* has its origins in Eastern and Western religions and philosophy. In Hinduism, for stance, the consequences of human actions—known as karma—are dictated by human interaction with the Earth and the universe. The same precept is found in all forms of Buddhism. It is also known that European Neolithic and Bronze Age societies warshiped Mother Earth through a number of female deities. Meanwhile, the ancient Greek worshiped the goddess Gaia as the ancestral mother of all life.

2. The Native-American Standing Rock Sioux Tribe took its flight for clean water all the way to the United Nations (UN). The tribe filed a lawsuit against the U.S. Army Corps of Engineers (USACE) after the agency permited construction of an oil pipeline from North Dakota to Illinois. The lawsuit asserted that the USACE had respected the National Historic Preservation Act and other laws. The UN, in response, called for a start in construction. It argued that the pipeline would be "a treat to drinking water supplies of the Standing Rock Sioux Tribe."

B. Make an argument for designating legal personhood to geographical features such as mountains, rivers, and seas. Your argument should contain your opinion as well as supporting facts and should be around 150 words.

Vocabulary in Context

A. Complete the conversation below with vocabulary from the passage.

| embryonic | intertwined | commodity | guardians | mayhem |

A: Maxie, all I can think about is the plummeting value of oil. It's not the best of times to be working at an energy company.

B: True. Oil is not a desired ....¹ these days. Neither is coal, I hear.

A: Everything is crazy in the energy markets at the moment. It's ....² !

B: Maybe you ought to switch jobs. You could work for a renewable energy provider.

A: The thing is, my company has just started producing renewable energy this year, but the project is still at an ....³ stage. That's why I don't want to leave.

B: Wow, has your company finally realized that our lives are ....⁴ with the environment we live in?

A: I don't think so. It's really a business decision. Management is starting to believe that there will be more profit from renewables in the future.

B: Oh, and they want to be viewed as the ....⁵ of renewables, right?

B. Choose the sentences where the underlined words have the same meanings as they do in the passage.

1.   a. Trina's nutritionist advised her to follow a strict dietary regime from now on.

   b. This country is suffering a dark period in its proud history due to a dictatorial regime.

2.   a. The memory of his father's love is enshrined forever in Nico's heart.

   b. The bodily remains of a famous saint are enshrined in the crypt of this small church.

3.   a. The school put the onus of providing scholarships on state funding rather than on itself.

   b. In criminal cases, the onus of proving a defendant's guilt falls on the prosecution.

C. Complete the chart below with definitions for the given phrases using "smooth." Then, write sentences using the phrases.

Phrases	Definitions
1. smooth as glass	*extremely smooth looking or smooth to the touch*
2. smooth operator	
3. smooth over	
4. smooth sailing	
5. smooth things out	

1. *The sea looked as **smooth as glass**; not a ripple could be seen across its immensity.*

2. ....

3. ....

4. ....

5. ....

Read the following passage on the Maori people. Then, do the exercises.

The Maori People

🎧 24

The Maori are the indigenous people of New Zealand. The Maori arrived there from eastern Polynesia between 1320 and 1350 by riding their oceangoing canoes. Due to New Zealand's geographical isolation, these early eastern Polynesian settlers developed a rather unique culture. Their language, crafts, mythology, music, and dances are distinct from those of other groups of Polynesian people.

The European arrival in New Zealand starting in the 17th century proved to be a mixed bag for the Maori. While they adopted many aspects of European culture and society, conflict and disease brought by European settlers led to the dramatic reduction of the Maori population. Diseases such as influenza and smallpox are believed to have killed as many as 50 percent of the Maori. Not until the 20th century had the Maori population begun to recover and efforts been made to guarantee social justice to the Maori.

The plight of the Maori to close the gap with the rest of New Zealand's ethnic groups, however, continues to this day. A lower life expectancy, fewer economic opportunities, subpar education, and high crime rates are all issues that continue to plague the Maori.

The Maori are also faced with an issue of identity. Prior to 1986, the New Zealand government identified a person as Maori based on a 50-percent Maori blood claim. Today, however, the government only requires some proof of ancestry or "continuing cultural connection" in order to define one as a Maori. In 2018, there were roughly 776,000 Maori in New Zealand, which was about 17 percent of the country's population. The Maori language is spoken to some degree by about 20 percent of Maori.

Making Inferences
Check (✓) the statements you think a Maori person would agree with.

1. The Maori are a distinct ethnic group in New Zealand, with their own language and customs. ☐

2. The European arrival in New Zealand in the 17th century was mostly beneficial to the Maori. ☐

3. The Maori continue to outpace New Zealand's other ethnic groups in quality of life standards. ☐

4. Currently, the Maori identity is defined by ancestry and connection to the Maori culture. ☐

5. Today, all Maori are able to fully appreciate and partake in all aspects of their culture. ☐

Reflections   Large corporations control large swaths of the Earth's lands, rivers, mountains, seas, and even oceans. Their actions have an oversized impact on ecosystems around the world and, consequently, on the health of our planet. Should corporations or even private individuals be allowed the right to ownership of oversized portions of the Earth? Should nature even be owned by humans?

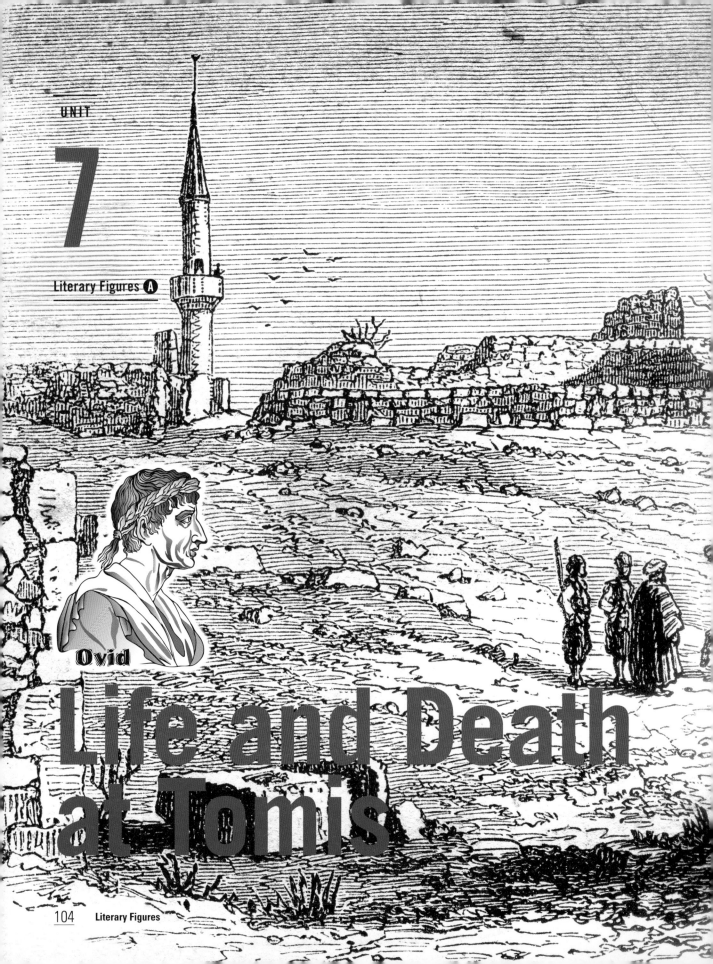

7

Literary Figures **Ⓐ**

Ovid

Life and Death at Tomis

Unit Preview

A. Discuss the following questions.

   1. Who are some famous figures of the Roman Empire that come to mind? Can you think of any famous Roman writers?

   2. Can you think of a person from your country who died while in exile in a foreign land?

B. Write definitions in English for the following words and expressions. Check your definitions again after reading the passage to make sure they fit the context of the passage.

   1. unbidden (*adj.*)

   2. unsolicited (*adj.*)

   3. dramatic monologue (*n.*)

   4. echelon (*n.*)

   5. libertine (*adj.*)

   6. bard (*n.*)

   7. ephemeral (*adj.*)

   8. reprieve (*n.*)

   9. wistful (*adj.*)

  10. furtively (*adv.*)

C. Test your knowledge on the topic of the exile of Roman poet Ovid at Tomis by checking Yes/No in the table below. After reading the passage, check whether your answers were correct or not.

Background Knowledge	True?	
	Yes	No
1. The Roman Empire stretched all the way to the Black Sea.		
2. Augustus was a famous Roman gladiator.		
3. *The Metamorphoses* was written by Roman poet Virgil.		

Ovidiu Square in the Old Town of Constanta, Romania

🎧 25

What did they mean?

1 Explain the following quote by Ovid: "It's a kindness that the mind can go where it wishes."

5

What did they mean?

2 Explain the following quote by Anthony McCarten: "Most writers live in self-imposed exile even when they don't leave their country."

10

15

The statue of Ovidius Naso

Poetry came natural to Publius Ovidius Naso (43 B.C. – 17 A.D.), one of ancient Rome's most linguistically and lyrically sophisticated poets. His penchant for lyrical verse came "unbidden" to Ovid, as the poet himself had stated in his letters. But if the Muses were indeed visiting Ovid unsolicited as he was gaining a following among Rome's beau monde[1], they would have been desperately summoned for company after the poet was booted in exile to the distant shores of Tomis, a settlement on the northeastern reaches of the empire.

Ovid rose to early Roman literary fame on the back of three early publishing successes: a collection of poems titled *Amores* (The Loves), which chronicled a fictional love affair with a woman named Corinna; a series of dramatic monologues titled *Heroides* (The Heroines), which catalogued the complexities of love experienced by famous women from mythology, such as Medea; and a collection of poems titled *Ars Amatoria* (The Art of Love), a three-part guide for men to successfully seduce women (the first two parts) and for women to successfully keep a man (the third part).

Ars Amatoria caused quite a stir[2] at the time of its publication, around 2 A.D. The erotic poems in this work represented Ovid's bold, often controversial reflection on the sexual practices of the time: "You ask perhaps if one should take the maid herself? / Such a plan brings the greatest risk with it. / In one case you're a prize for her mistress, in the other herself." The frank, instructional tone of these verses earned Ovid an enthusiastic readership, especially among Rome's young, affluent groups, propelling the 42-year-old poet into the upper echelons of Roman society.

The libertine nature of the *Ars Amatoria* poems unfortunately also brought an unwanted source of scrutiny upon Ovid's work: Emperor Augustus, who had been championing a moral lifestyle. For the time being, Ovid avoided the emperor's wrath and instead turned his creative attention to his next literary project: *The Metamorphoses,* an epic collection of some 250 captivating poems that retell the stories of mythical and mortal characters from Greek and Latin antiquity.

By 8 A.D., Ovid had reached the peak of his literary fame, being counted alongside Virgil and Horace as one of the greatest bards of Latin literature. But in the eternal city of Rome, life was paradoxically ephemeral. And Ovid would learn this hard truth himself when Augustus ordered him away due to what Ovid had only enigmatically referred to as a "*carmen et error*" (a poem and an error). Both the identity of the poem and the nature of the error committed remain a hotly debated mystery to this day.

What is certain is that at the age of 50, Ovid bid farewell to his friends and family and swapped his extravagant Roman living for a primitive life on the shores of the Black Sea at Tomis, where "barbarians kept out the dreadful cold with sewn trousers and furs." The despair that accompanied Ovid's daily struggles in these lands are chronicled in his heart-wrenching poems of exile, collected in two books titled *Tristia* (Lamentations) and *Epistulae ex Ponto* (Black Sea Letters). To the very end, Ovid kept up hope for a return to his dear Rome: "Our native soil draws all of us—I know not by what sweetness—and never allows us to forget."

Ovid's reprieve never did come. Instead, hope grew ever dimmer, and as darkness descended upon him, Ovid became a wistful reminder of how furtively humanity can be undone by a death-in-life in exile: "Writing a poem you can read to no one is like dancing in the dark."

What did they mean?

3 Explain the following quote by Richard von Weizsaecker: "Seeking to forget makes exile all the longer; the secret of redemption lies in remembrance."

An old Romanian stamp with the image of Ovid

→ **IDIOMS: Usage and Etymology** ←

1 **beau monde:** This idiom comes from the French language and literally means "the beautiful people" and figuratively means "society's wealthiest and most fashionable." The expression has been used since the Georgian period (early 18th century), when the emerging European middle class aspired to and emulated the extravagant lifestyles of the aristocracy.

2 **cause a stir:** This idiom has the figurative meaning of "inciting trouble, interest, or excitement." The verb "stir" finds its origin in the old English *styrian*, meaning "agitate" or "incite," while the noun "stir" derives from old Norse *styrr*, meaning "disturbance" or "tumult."

Reading Comprehension

Choose the best answers to the following questions on the passage "Life and Death at Tomis."

Inference

1. Where in the passage would the following sentence fit best?

"Sometimes in life, hope doesn't lead to a positive outcome:"

a. at the beginning of the first paragraph

b. at the beginning of the fourth paragraph

c. at the beginning of the fifth paragraph

d. at the beginning of the last paragraph

Did You Know? ∞∞∞∞∞∞∞

Civitas—full Roman citizenship—was the prize of a few (not given to women, slaves, etc.) and the envy of many. A Roman citizen could vote, hold office, own property, had the right to a trial in Rome, and could never be killed on a cross (crucified).

Detail

2. Which of the following books most likely angered Emperor Augustus?

a. *Ars Amatoria*

b. *The Metamorphoses*

c. *Tristia*

d. *Epistulae ex Ponto*

Detail

3. Which of the following was NOT a topic explored by Ovid in his works?

a. a chronicle of a fictional love affair

b. an exploration of the time's sexual practices

c. an error committed against Emperor Augustus

d. the lament and despair experienced in exile

Did You Know? ∞∞∞∞∞∞∞

The Colosseum in Rome was sometimes the site of reenactments of large boat battles, complete with warriors battling each other—and crocodiles— in water.

Vocabulary

4. Which word pair does NOT fit in with the others?

a. joyous / heart-wrenching

b. extravagant / primitive

c. erotic / romantic

d. eternal / ephemeral

Vocabulary

5. Which of the following is synonymous with the highlighted word in paragraph 1?

a. hired

b. taken in

c. expelled

d. allowed

Inference

6. Which of the following statements can be inferred from the passage?

a. Ovid's books *Tristia* and *Epistulae ex Ponto* enjoyed huge success in Tomis.

b. The affluent class in Roman society was not exactly morally upright.

c. Due to his exile, Ovid has been forgotten by literature and history.

d. Ovid was used to living a modest life in Rome prior to his exile.

Inference

7. Which of the following best relates to the theme of this passage?

a. "Life begins on the other side of despair." (Jean Paul Sartre)

b. "Some men fall from grace. Some are pushed." (Jim Butcher)

c. "Your birth is a mistake you'll spend your whole life trying to correct." (Chuck Palahniuk)

d. "Women may fall when there's no strength in men." (William Shakespeare)

Proofreading and Writing Practice

A. Read the following passages. Find 5 mistakes in each paragraph and correct them.

1. The contents of Ovid's book *Ars Amatoria* were ~~severe~~ *severely* at odds with Emperor Augustus's conservative views on societal norms of behavior. Augustus exiled his own daughter, Julia, for precisely the kinds of behavior described in Ovid's book. The fact that Augustus would embrace members of his own family demonstrates that he had no patience for Romans who engaged in debauchery. Whatever mistake Ovid made to push Augustus over the edge did not, to itself, cause the poet's exile. One can argue that due to his libertine writings, Ovid's exile was a long times coming.

2. Much has been made about the mature of the error made by Ovid to warrant his exile by Emperor Augustus. Suggestions have been made of a possible romantic quarrel between Ovid and the emperor's wife or maybe even his daughter. Others have proposed that Ovid had witness some private aspect of the emperor's life. In *Tristia*, Ovid writes the following intrigue lines: "I said nothing, my tongue never shaped words of violence, / no seditious impieties escaped me in my cups. / Unwitting, I witnesed a crime: for that I'm afflicted: / my offence is that I had eyes."

B. Make an argument for a case when societies need to exile their citizens. Your argument should contain your opinion as well as supporting facts and should be around 150 words.

Vocabulary in Context

A. Complete the conversation below with vocabulary from the passage.

| bard | dramatic monologue | ephemeral | furtively | reprieve | wistful |

A: What are you reading there, Marco?

B: "The Love Song of J. Alfred Prufrock," a poem by T.S. Eliot. It's a .... [1] because it represents the thoughts of a fictional character.

A: Ah, Eliot, the great modernist .... [2]. Is it interesting?

B: It makes me think about the .... [3] nature of life and its ceaseless passing.

A: Yeah, so it's pretty depressing then. And speaking of depressing thoughts, what's that word for when you feel a regretful longing for something?

B: .... [4]. Do you feel a longing for something?

A: Yeah, a glass of wine. For Eliot, you know. You must keep some wine around the house, ... [5] stashed away in some cabinet, I'm sure...

B: No wine for you. The poetry gods are punishing you for making light of it.

A: But you have the power to give me a .... [6]! Come on. A glass of vino!

Did You Know? ◇◇◇◇◇◇◇◇◇◇

The term "Pyrrhic victory" comes from the victory by Greek King Pyrrhus over Rome. This first military encounter between Roman legion and Macedonian phalanx units resulted in unsustainable losses for the Greeks, making it a "fruitless victory."

B. Choose the sentences where the underlined words have the same meanings as they do in the passage.

1. a. In just a matter of minutes, some 20 underbidden guests showed up at Jeff's party.

   b. Always at the end of this movie, unbidden tears inevitably come to Jeannie's eyes.

2. a. While not yet 20, Mark had already reached the highest echelon of the fashion world.

   b. A formation of F-22 Raptors zipped across the sky in a fearsome echelon.

3. a. Even in this day and age, his views are rather libertine for a Catholic priest.

   b. Oscar Wilde was ultimately sent to jail for his libertine lifestyle.

C. Complete the chart below with definitions for the given phrases using "dead." Then, write sentences using the phrases.

Phrases	Definitions
1. dead ringer	*one who looks exactly like someone else*
2. dead set against	
3. dead to the world	
4. dead in the water	
5. deadpan face	

Did You Know? ◇◇◇◇◇◇◇◇◇◇

The inscription made by Emperor Trajan on the bridge over the Tagus River in Spain reads, "I have built a bridge that will last forever." Indeed, the Roman bridge still stands and is in use today.

1. *Kim Jeong-un was shown in a picture with a **dead ringer** that looked uncannily like him.*

2. ....

3. ....

4. ....

5. ....

Read the following passage on Tomis and the Black Sea. Then, do the exercises.

Myth and Modernity
on the Black Sea

🎧 26

The modern city of Constanta, located on the Romanian coast on the Black Sea, sits on the remains of the old Roman settlement Tomis. The origin of the name Tomis comes from a rather tragic Greek legend. We are told that the beautiful princess Medea flees her father, taking along her little brother Absirt. Their father, King Aeetes, vows to catch and punish Medea for her rebelliousness. As the father's ship approaches her own, Medea brutally chops Absirt into pieces and scatters his body parts at sea, hoping that it will slow down the father long enough for her to escape. The grieving king does slow down to collect the pieces of his son and then moors his boat on the nearest shore to give Absirt a proper burial. A city is later built on this shore and is given the name Tomis by the Greeks, meaning "pieces." In real life, the shores of Tomis did become home to a number of distant visitors through the ages. The Phoenicians settled down here in the first millennium B.C. They were followed by the Greeks and the Romans, who built up the city and expanded its outside trade, as well as an assortment of barbarians who tore it down, relegating its structures to the dustbin of history.

The city of Constanta was built not far from the ruins of Tomis by Roman Emperor Constantine the Great, and subsequent visits by Genovese sailors, who made it part of their trading routes, added to its urban and commercial development until the Turkish conquest, when the city sank into its darkest period. Today, Constanta is the largest port on the Black Sea and the fourth largest port in Europe after Rotterdam, Antwerp, and Marseille. The temperate climate of this region—a far cry from Ovid's description of a frozen land where "barbarians cover themselves with furs"—makes Constanta and its satellite resort cities on the Romanian Black Sea coast a favorite summer destination for flocks of Northern European tourists seeking to vacation on their sun-soaked beaches.

In recent years, old Tomis has welcomed yet another distant visitor to its shores: the U.S. Army, which has established a military base at nearby Mihail Kogalniceanu Airport, hoping to turn the old Roman outpost region into a bulwark for NATO's defenses on its eastern approaches.

Making Inferences
Check (✓) the statements you think a citizen of Constanta would agree with.

1. The modern city of Constanta is as inhospitable as its historical urban ancestor, Tomis. ☐

2. The beaches of Constanta and nearby resort cities welcome many European vacationers. ☐

3. The Turks did to Constanta what the barbarians had done to Tomis. ☐

4. Today, Constanta outranks all of Europe's trade hubs, including Rotterdam, Antwerp, and Marseille. ☐

5. Ovid symbolically shared Absirt's fate: the broken pieces of his heart were buried in Tomis. ☐

Reflections   Some practitioners of religions, such as Buddhist monks, may undertake self-exile in order to achieve a higher state of spirituality. But self-imposed exiles may not be that different from forced exiles; in a sense, both can lead to a period of introspection that involves personal growth. Looking at exiles from this perspective, should these experiences be part of everyone's life?

Juan Rulfo:
Not Speaking
for the Dead

Unit Preview

A. Discuss the following questions.

   1. Who is your favorite international writer? Can you name any Latin American writers?

   2. What is your favorite novel written by any of the writers mentioned in question 1?

B. Write definitions in English for the following words and expressions. Check your definitions again after reading the passage to make sure they fit the context of the passage.

   1. oblige (*v.*) _____

   2. pry one's hand loose (*phr.*) _____

   3. spirited (*adj.*) _____

   4. brevity (*n.*) _____

   5. reticent (*adj.*) _____

   6. secular (*adj.*) _____

   7. firing squad (*n.*) _____

   8. impressionable (*adj.*) _____

   9. parched (*adj.*) _____

   10. whip up (*phr.*) _____

C. Test your knowledge on the topic of Mexican writer Juan Rulfo by checking Yes/No in the table below. After reading the passage, check whether your answers were correct or not.

Background Knowledge	True?	
	Yes	No
1. Juan Rulfo is considered one of the greatest Mexican writers.		
2. Juan Rulfo wrote a large number of novels and short story collections.		
3. Juan Rulfo's *Pedro Páramo* is a novel about the nobility of the human spirit.		

You can always know a masterful novel from its opening lines—the way it grabs hold of you like a mugger in a dark alley and demands everything in exchange for your life. All you can do at that point is to oblige it and to keep reading until it is finished with you. The novel *Pedro Páramo* by arguably Mexico's greatest writer, Juan Rulfo (1917-1986), is such a novel. Consider its opening lines: "I came to Comala because I was told that my father, a certain Pedro Páramo, was living there. My mother told me so, and I promised her I would come to see him as soon as she died... all I could do was to keep telling her I would do it, and I kept on saying it until I had to pry my hand loose from her dead fingers."

Juan Rulfo was by no means a prolific writer. His main works are a collection of short stories titled *El Llano en Llamas* (1953) and the novel *Pedro Páramo* (1955), and between them, these books come to roughly 300 pages of writing. But these 300 pages have the spirited power of the 300 Spartans that stopped an empire. Rulfo's pages had been called by Nobel Prize-winning novelist Gabriel García Márquez "as durable as the pages that have come down to us from Sophocles."

The brevity of words in Rulfo's writings mirrored his reticent real-life personality, due perhaps to his traumatic childhood: Born in the restless western Mexican state of Jalisco, young Rulfo witnessed all the terror of the Cristero Rebellion (1926-1929), a revolt of the rural inhabitants against a secular government that had started the persecution of Catholic priests. The horror that unfolded before Rulfo's eyes must have been a powerful reason for his characteristic silence: men— sometimes neighbors—were abducted, beaten, dragged before firing squads, strung up and hanged, and much more.

Rulfo's own family fared no better during these times: his father, a grandfather, and several

What did they mean?

1 Explain the following quote from *Pedro Páramo*: "They say that when people from there die and go to hell, they come back for a blanket."

What did they mean?

2 Explain the following quote from *Pedro Páramo*: "The road rose and fell. It rises or falls whether you're coming or going. If you are leaving, it's uphill; but as you arrive, it's downhill."

other relatives were murdered while his mother died due to a heart issue. Watching the whole world come apart at the seams[1] around him, young Rulfo found a much-needed source of sanity in the library of books donated to his family by the local priest before leaving to join the Cristero Rebellion. The books must have convinced Rulfo at that impressionable age and in those moments of absolute savagery that any present or future salvation must be found in the pages of books.

Juan Rulfo is one of the greatest Latin American writer of the 20th century.

In Rulfo's novel, Juan Preciado, the protagonist of the story, is headed to Comala to meet his father, Pedro Páramo. Comala is a parched town where a lone woman named Eduviges Dyada lives surrounded by ghost neighbors. Dyada offers lodging to Juan, and as he starts walking around the town, he soon uncovers disquieting facts about his father: how, drunk on power, he turned Comala into a burial ground and destroyed everyone in the process, including his own children and the woman he loved. The reader eventually realizes that Juan has been dead from the very start and that he has been narrating the whole story from a coffin he shares with his former nanny, a salt-of-the-earth[2] woman who wanted to be his mother.

Pedro Páramo is a novel populated by characters who feel abandoned by all hope and by God himself. This is a novel that remains as relevant today as it was in the 1950s, forcing contemplation on how to face the death and destruction whipped up by the brutal strongmen and dictators of our time without giving in to the despair that follows in its aftermath. Juan Rulfo's life of self-imposed silence was as powerful a statement as are the clasped hands in death of those that will forever not let their struggle go.

What did they mean?

3 Explain the following quote from *Pedro Páramo*: "Not a breath. I had to suck in the same air I exhaled, cupping it in my hands before it escaped. I felt it, in and out, less each time, until it was so thin, it slipped through my fingers forever."

→ **IDIOMS: Usage and Etymology** ←

1 **come apart at the seams:** This idiom has the figurative meaning of "disintegrating or falling apart" when used with an object and "having an emotional breakdown" when used with people. The idiom was first used as slang in the mid-1900s, when it alluded to something physically falling apart to refer to a falling apart in an emotional sense.

2 **salt-of-the-earth:** This idiom has the figurative meaning of "having great value or importance." The Biblical phrase derives from Christ's Sermon on the Mount to the common people: "You are the salt of the earth." (Matthew 5:13) The meaning was that these fishermen, shepherds, and laborers were as worthy and virtuous as salt, which was a valuable commodity in those days.

Reading Comprehension

Choose the best answers to the following questions on the passage "Juan Rulfo: Not Speaking for the Dead."

Inference 1. **Where in the passage would the following sentence fit best?**

"And it must've set his heart to writing."

a. at the end of the second paragraph

b. at the end of the third paragraph

c. at the end of the fourth paragraph

d. at the end of the fifth paragraph

Detail 2. **Which of the following is NOT the name of a fictional character?**

a. Pedro Paramo

b. Juan Preciado

c. Gabriel García Márquez

d. Eduviges Dyada

Detail 3. **Which of the following statements about Juan Rulfo is true?**

a. He was a Nobel Prize-winning novelist.

b. He was told that his father was living in Comala.

c. He was deeply affected by the horrors of the Cristero Rebellion.

d. His self-imposed silence was a protest against the Cristero rebels.

Vocabulary 4. **Which word pairs or phrase does NOT fit in with the others?**

a. drunk on power

b. savage strongmen

c. brutal dictators

d. traumatic childhood

Vocabulary 5. **Which of the following is an antonym of the highlighted word in paragraph 5?**

a. reassuring   b. alarming   c. distressing   d. disturbing

Inference 6. **Which of the following statements can be inferred from the passage?**

a. *Pedro Páramo* is a horror story that lacks a factual basis and real-life relevance.

b. The novel *Pedro Páramo* draws heavily from Juan Rulfo's life experiences.

c. Juan Rulfo's own father was a ruthless and sinful strongman.

d. The characters of *Pedro Páramo* are spirited in their resolve to maintain hope.

Inference 7. **Which of the following best relates to the theme of *Pedro Páramo*?**

a. "The mob is the most ruthless of tyrants." (Friedrich Nietzsche)

b. "The distrust of wit is the beginning of tyranny." (Edward Abbey)

c. "A city which belongs to just one man is no true city." (Sophocles)

d. "Tyranny is always better organized than freedom." (Charles Péguy)

Proofreading and Writing Practice

A. Read the following passages. Find 5 mistakes in each paragraph and correct them.

1. The Cristero Rebellion was a power tussle ~~among~~ *between* the Mexican government and the Catholic Church. In July 31, 1926, President Plutarco Elias Calles called for all Catholic clerics to submit to the Calles Law, which called for the enforcement of anticlerical policies set fourth in the Mexican Constitution of 1917. Among these policies was the prohibition of the Catholic Church from owing property. The Calles Law also called to the government to nationalize all church buildings, outlawed religious houses, and banned public religious functions. Additionally, it declared priests to register in order to avoid fines or imprisonment.

2. Juan Rulfo's disdain for speaking was famous. One day, Antonio Skármeta, the reader of *Il Postino*, saw Jorge Luis Borges and Juan Rulfo coming out of a Buenos Aires radio studio. On seeing Borges, Skármeta asked, "How does it go, maestro?" The reply from Borges was, "Very well indeed. I talked and talked, and often in a while, Rulfo intervened with a moment of silence." Rulfo objected with Borges's explanation by simply nodding his head.

B. Make an argument for the separation of powers between government and religion. Your argument should contain your opinion as well as supporting facts and should be around 150 words.

Vocabulary in Context

A. Complete the conversation below with vocabulary from the passage.

firing squad	reticent	pry my hand loose	whipped up	parched

A: I heard from Ari that you believe that aliens are abducting people. Or is this just a rumor that Ari _____¹?

B: They are. Some people disappear for weeks without explanation, and then they reappear like they've never been gone. Where do they go?

A: Maybe on a vacation to Hawaii?

B: I hope they take you, too, for your bad jokes.

A: They'd have to _____² from my shotgun. They maybe they'd stand a chance.

B: Oh, of course, because you're a one-man _____³, and an advanced race will just line up against a wall and wait for you to execute them.

A: I preferred when you were _____⁴. Too much talking doesn't fit your style all that well.

B: Too much talk indeed. My mouth is _____⁵. Let's get a drink!

A: Agreed. Let's forget all this alien drivel.

Did You Know? ◇◇◇◇◇◇◇◇◇◇◇◇◇◇

Juan Rulfo worked as a traveling salesman from 1946 to 1952. The position demanded long driving trips across southern Mexico. When Rulfo asked for a radio for his company car in 1952, he was fired. That year, he received a writing fellowship supported by the Rockefeller Foundation and started writing *Pedro Páramo*. Sometimes it pays off to be fired from a job.

B. Choose the sentences where the underlined words have the same meanings as they do in the passage.

1.   a. "I would be much <u>obliged</u> if you could put in a good word for me," he requested kindly.

   b. The mother made her request known, and her two sons <u>obliged</u> without further comment.

2.   a. Jane Goodall is a <u>spirited</u> advocate for animal rights.

   b. I wouldn't say he's mean <u>spirited</u>, but then again, I wouldn't say he isn't.

3.   a. The new government has exhibited less <u>secular</u> attitudes toward religion.

   b. This kind of economic upheaval is a rare, almost <u>secular</u> phenomenon.

C. Complete the chart below with definitions for the given phrases using "walk." Then, write sentences using the phrases.

Phrases	Definitions
1. walk of life	*an occupation; a role; a social class; a lifestyle*
2. walk on eggs	
3. walk on the wild side	
4. walk the line	
5. walk the walk	

Did You Know? ◇◇◇◇◇◇◇◇◇◇

Jalisco, the home state of Juan Rulfo, gave birth to Mariachi music, the wide-brimmed sombrero hat, and the popular tequila drink.

1. *Britta was literally born into her unique **walk of life**: circus performer.*

2. _____

3. _____

4. _____

5. _____

Read the following passage on magical realism in literature. Then, do the exercises.

 *Magical Realism in Literature* 🎧 28

Magical realism is a literary genre that spins elements of fantasy and myth into stories of everyday life. In the world of magical realism, the boundary between the real and the imagined is often concealed. Here, the ordinary becomes extraordinary quite matter-of-factly while the magical becomes commonplace with equal nonchalance.

The term "magical realism" can be applied to various forms of fiction: short stories, novels, poetry, plays, and films. The term, however, is also used in art, where it can describe realistic and figurative paintings, drawings, and sculptures as well as other works of art that imply hidden meanings in their messages.

The start of Latin American magical realism in literature is often attributed to a story written in 1935 by Jorge Luis Borges (1899-1986), an Argentinian writer. But magical realism traces its roots to Europe, when Frantz Kafka (1883-1924), a Czech writer of Jewish descent, wrote the story "The Metamorphosis" in 1912.

While other European writers, such as Italo Calvino and Günter Grass, produced literary works that weaved fantasy with reality, this style of writing was more widely adopted in the second half of the 20th century by the Latin American writers that followed in the footsteps of Jorge Luis Borges. These included Juan Rulfo (1917-1986), Gabriel García Márquez (1927-2014), Isabel Allende (born 1942), and Paulo Coelho (born 1947).

Today, magical realism is a truly international phenomenon, finding expression in countries from Japan to the United States, with writers such as Saint Lucian Derek Walcott (1930-2017) and Japanese Haruki Murakami (born in 1949) being recognized for their masterful use of this style with the Nobel Prize in Literature.

Making Inferences
Check (✓) the statements you think a literary critic would agree with.

1. In the world of magical realism, realism is unquestionably separated from the fantastic. ☐

2. The true masters of magical realism were European writers such as Kafka and Calvino. ☐

3. The term "magical realism" is restricted to works of literature such as novels and films. ☐

4. Magical realism was more widely adopted by Latin American writers than European ones. ☐

5. Today, writers from Asian countries are also writing in the magical realist style. ☐

Reflections   There is no doubt that Juan Rulfo possessed writing ability in his native Spanish language that was brilliant. The English translations of his works, however, have masked to a certain degree his literary genius. When comparing the great minds of literature, do writers who write in English, such as Derek Walcott, enjoy an advantage over writers who rely on English translations of their works, such as Juan Rulfo? It should be noted that Rulfo never won the Nobel Prize in Literature while Walcott did, yet Rulfo has enjoyed far wider recognition across all cultures and languages than Walcott.